TIM BIRD
INGALILL SNITT
JUHANI PALLASMAA

Living in
FINLAND

Flammarion

CONTENTS

Facing page: Sophisticated simplicity and familiarity with wood, Finland's most abundant natural material, are characteristics of Finnish building design. Details are from a house in Porvoo (top left), the Villa Uunila (top right and bottom left), and a street in the town of Rauma (bottom right).

INTERNALIZED LANDSCAPE

JUHANI PALLASMAA

"Like the Almighty Himself, we make everything in our image, for want of a more reliable model; our artifacts tell more about ourselves than our confessions," states Joseph Brodsky.[1]

Culture weaves together countless collective responses, mental images and value judgements, and these features are materialized in our artifacts and architecture. Although we usually sense cultural differences of the human landscape intuitively, we are hardly able to describe these characteristics in words. We grasp the essences of lived situations without consciously understanding them.

Like poetry and painting, architecture and design are engaged in articulating and expressing existential meanings. All art forms create spatial, formal, or material metaphors of our basic existential encounters with landscape and climate, history and tradition. These lived metaphors of art are highly abstracted and compressed forms that fuse a multitude of experiences into singular images. Artistic works are microcosms, condensed representations of the experiential life-world.

What are the constituents of the "Finnishness" of Finnish architecture and design? Finland is the most forested country in Europe, and our lifestyle and artistic culture are bound to reflect this condition. The landscape of the Finnish mindset continues to be the forest. We may well live in modern cities today, but the imagery of the forest still occupies our very souls. Even in the era of globalization, mobility, exchange, and digital realities, we desire to return back to the embrace of the forest. Most of us Finns deliberately reject the condition of modern urban life in the summertime, and revert back to the lifestyle of the primordial forest dweller. In fact, during the short summer weeks at our summer huts, we present entirely different personalities than during the long winter months in cities. We become forest people, hunter-gatherers, and fishermen again.

The forest condition emphasizes primary causalities of life and the multisensory nature of experience, and it brings forth a haptic intimacy. This is a landscape where sounds, tactile experiences, muscular and skeletal imageries of motion, smells and suggestions of taste balance the dominance of vision characteristic to Western urban cultures.

Landscape, climate, and the cyclic rhythms of seasons mould human character. Even the senses are tuned for particular nuances by the characteristics of one's childhood environment. Throughout our lives, we experience places and landscapes through the memory of our childhood world. The sense of domicile and home is deeply rooted; the structuring and utilization of space is guided by the hidden geometries of our mother tongue.

The landscape also acquires symbolic content and significance. The forest, with its mythological and imaginary qualities and mythical inhabitants, has a central role in the Finnish psyche. The Finnish therapist Pirkko Siltala describes the interrelationship between the Finnish mentality and the forest: "Man internalizes his external surroundings, [...] as an internal landscape of the soul, a forest of the soul [...]. We feel the forest is like our father's or mother's body. The primal response of the body, the language of the senses, is brought to life in both the mother's

The imagery of Finnish art, architecture, and design reflects the patterns, structures, rhythms, and colors of the northern forest (preceding page). Finns seek the solitude, silence, and harmony provided by natural settings (left). The simplicity and restraint of Finnish formal expression reflects ethical attitudes (facing page).

and the forest's embrace. But then we also externalize our internal thoughts, feelings, passions, fears, erotic fantasies, and desires into the forest."[2]

The impact of the forest can be distinguished in the motifs of Finnish literature, painting, and music as well as architecture and design. We can distinguish a distinct 'forest poetry', a "forest art," as well as a "music of the forest" which is well exemplified by the naturalistic air of Jean Sibelius' music.

Regardless of cultural interactions and today's technological refinements, Finnish aesthetic sensibilities are grounded in the peasant mode of life that persists in our collective memory. The timeless aesthetics of necessity in farm life, and the ideal of "noble poverty" have turned into the modern aesthetics of restraint. Simplicity is an ethical attitude rather than a stylistic and visual preference.

However, describing Finnish aesthetic ideals solely as a reflection of the Nordic nature, or primordial peasant traditions would be a simplification. All cultures assimilate influences from others and these creative amalgamations of external influences in the arts are often amazingly complex. The Finnish style of life, as well as art, keeps fusing influences from other cultures with layers of indigenous Finnish history and the prevailing naturalistic attitude.

Traditionally we Finns prefer silence over clatter, restraint over exuberance, and slowness over haste. These preferences emphasize utilitarian and functional practicalities over artificial, decorative, or self-expressive aims. In our culture even individualistic expression tends to acknowledge the boundaries of a collective canon. Moderation, temperance, and reservedness are regarded as virtues in social behaviour as well as in art, design, and architecture. This combined attachment to nature and an unpretentious practicality gives rise to a lyrical pragmatism. Primordial pantheistic view of nature is fused with a matter-of-factness.

For the inhabitants of the northern latitudes, light is a precious gift. In a country of lakes, snow, and ice, light is often reflected from below, or it may turn into an illuminated mist or glowing matter. Light is the most subtle of all media of artistic expression; light can communicate grief or bliss, melancholy or joy, nostalgia or ecstasy. Light mediates between matter and spirit. On my frequent travels on other continents, the last image in my mind's eyes before falling asleep, is often a counterlight reflected through a forest from the shimmering surface of a forest lake.

[1] Joseph Brodsky, *Watermark*, Penguin Books, London and New York, 1992, 61.

[2] Pirkko Siltala, "Metsän turvallisuus" [The security of the forest], *Silva Fennica* 21, No. 4 (1987): 406–13.

INTRODUCTION

IN HARMONY WITH NATURE

In one of his rare recorded interviews, Jean Sibelius (1865–1957), one of Finland's best-known and most loved sons, was asked what his advice would be to a young, aspiring composer. His response was that one should consistently avoid the use of unnecessary notes, because "every note should have a life of its own."

There is something essentially Finnish about this proposal. This is a nation that has little time for the superfluous. Waste is scorned, and airs and graces do not impress. It would be easy to interpret these traits as a lack of appreciation of the joys of life and leisure, but the Finns, with their saunas, lakeside holiday retreats, and sailing boats, have clear ideas about how to make the most of their environment.

Environment defines all nations to some extent, but the Finns have a closer affinity than most with their geographical and climatic circumstances. The unspoiled environment—the wide, placid lakes, the forest and wildlife, and the rugged coastline—is what attracts many visitors from abroad, and the high Finnish standard of living is reflected in the invariable quality of accommodation. The Finnish lifestyle is one that demands comfort and efficiency, while shunning the ostentatious and flamboyant.

The Finnish celebration of simplicity and functionality is a source of pride and an asset,it is at the root of its most renowned achievements and reflected in its international success stories. The Finnish economy is repeatedly identified as one of the world's most competitive, and its global brands—from Fiskars to Nokia—are household names and market leaders.

At the same time, its artistic expressions, from the architecture of Aalto to the opera of Kaija Saariaho, have left a signature whose boldness is out of proportion to the country's small population. Yet the full range of accomplishments, from the industrial to the aesthetic, spring from a shared source of creative, concerted practicality.

Finland's handicap has been multiplied by the unchangeable fact of its location, flung to the north of Europe and separated from it by the Baltic Sea. Traditionally a pawn in international political power games and a prize of combat between the historical imperial powers—first Sweden, then Russia—the Finnish character has been hardened in part by the determination to retain a national identity. The neat new towns of modern Finland are also a modern phenomenon and the rigors of the rural forest lifestyle remain embedded in the Finn's psychology.

The Finns have a name—*sisu*—for the element of their character that has evolved from these circumstances: a self-perceived quality of grit and gutsy persistence. It is *sisu*, they say, that underlines their Finnishness, defining their approach to the world. They attribute it to their sporting heroes—the Olympic champions Paavo Nurmi and Lasse Virén, the ski jumpers, the Formula One and rally drivers—as much as to their military and historical icons, such as Mannerheim and Kekkonen. It found its ultimate manifestation in their two most recent wars with the giant eastern neighbor, Russia: the Winter War of 1939–1940 and the Continuation War of 1941–1944. In these conflicts, Finland was David to the Soviet Goliath—universally admired as plucky and heroic, and, although it ultimately had to pay the price by ceding a large portion of eastern territory to the Soviet Union, it gained the reward of post-war independence that its Baltic neighbors, for example, could not share.

Having passed through the era of cautious neutrality that followed the war, Finland finds itself much more at ease in—and committed to—its contemporary European setting. The incentives for communication skills in other languages are obvious for the Finns and a traditionally modest reluctance to put these skills into practice is much less evident with every passing year. Finns are good linguists, but not at the expense of their own distinctive tongue, which thrives and adapts, feeding on loans from other languages without sacrificing its own complex idioms and grammar.

The Finns are among the most literate, widely read, and well-informed nations on Earth. Their population of 5.3 million has access to a phenomenal range of media: 200 newspapers, some 2,400 popular and specialist magazines, about 70 commercial radio stations, and a selection of TV channels, national and international, that multiplies weekly. Finland consistently figures among the top five countries in terms of Internet access. This is a land that thrives on information; it is also both a pioneer and an enthusiastic adopter of the technology that distributes it.

Finnish life in the twenty-first century is a phenomenal combination of the modern and the traditional, where technological opportunities and applications are relished, yet where basic values run deep. In the face of real and difficult challenges—of geography, of climate, of history, and of language—the Finns progress in quiet triumph, less reticent about their own achievements, but more confident that these achievements speak loudly for themselves.

BEAUTY IN WOOD
The traditional Finnish wooden milieu, such as that of the Kirsti house in Rauma (right), has a charming, functional beauty, which is emphasized by the softening effect of thick snow in winter. Old wooden quarters survive alongside Finland's neat modern towns. The kick sled shown here is of a type still used in rural areas as a means of getting around.

LANDSCAPES

In a Western world that is slowly awakening to find itself parched and gasping in an urban desert, Finland has found itself attracting attention as an oasis of natural beauty. First-time visitors are often surprised by what they find. The sheer size of Finland, for instance, is often a revelation: it measures some 810 miles (1,300 km) from the southern Baltic tip to the northern fells above the Arctic Circle. The total population of just over five million occupies an area that is about the same size as the US state of Montana and bigger than that of the United Kingdom. Space is plentiful. Finnish space means lake systems that meander toward a wide horizon and an infinite carpet of forest.

To live in Finland is to accept the full range of climatic extremes, through the spiteful Baltic wind and rain, the steely frosts and blizzards, to the absolute clarity of its winter skies, and the enchanted stubborn light and drowsy warmth of its summer evenings. Finnish winters can be as cruel as they are exhilarating, while Finnish summers can be magnificent. To experience life in one of Europe's most northerly countries is to have the opportunity to appreciate the balance between the seasons and the cycles of nature in a way that has become more difficult elsewhere in Europe.

The natural environment is also more subtly varied than many might expect. True, the themes of forest, lake, and rock are repeated to some

HANKO
*The southern archipelago landscape in the vicinity of the port
of Hanko is at once intimate and expansive. Rowanberries
add splashes of color to the shoreline landscape (far left),
and in the town the domes of the Orthodox Church, dedicated
to St. Vladimir, scrape a pure blue sky (left). Shelves of granite
(facing page), smoothed by centuries of ice and storms, provide
flawless mirrors to the sky.*

BIRCH TREES
*Birch trees by a Finnish lake provide a natural washing line.
The Finns are at home and at ease in the tranquil beauty
of their natural environment (page 14).*

extent in almost every corner of the country, and the spectacular scope of the landscape is derived from this vast continuity. But increasing familiarity with the country leads to a recognition of its regional elements. The forest, with its predominant species of pine, spruce, and birch, is dark and mysterious in places, sparse and airy in others. The rocks swoop and slide along the coasts and islands, but rear up in dangerous crags throughout the ridges and gorges of the inland north.

Forests, lakes, coasts, and rivers are also the source of Finland's simple cuisine. Forest floors are thick with blueberries, lingonberries, cloudberries, raspberry canes, and aromatic wild strawberries, as well as chanterelle and boletus mushrooms. The woods are also host to a variety of game, from elk to grouse, and the waters teem with salmon, perch, and zander. The Finns are modest about their gastronomic resources, but the fresh ingredients of the forests are facets of the Finnish lifestyle. The continued assertion of "Everyman's rights" enshrines the rights of every Finn—and every visitor—to wander and camp freely in the forests and to gather the wild berries and mushrooms in unrestricted areas.

The southern province of Uusimaa—literally, "new country"—is the most densely populated area of Finland, containing the capital, Helsinki, and its surrounding and expanding conurbation, as well as a corridor of towns hugging the main railway artery down to the coast. Helsinki, founded in 1550 in commercial competition to the Estonian capital, Tallinn, fifty miles (80 km) across the Gulf of Finland, is the country's biggest port. It straddles a cluster of islands and promontories on Finland's southern, most temperate tip, now a little closer to the sea than its original location at the mouth of the Vantaa river.

The city sits at the middle of a community of major Baltic cities, from majestic Saint Petersburg in the east to quaint, medieval Tallinn in the south, and sparkling Stockholm to the west. The Gulf of Finland and the rest of the Baltic are a vital part of the national geographical and mental landscape, since they represent the biggest natural barrier between Finland and the rest of Europe. Even so, since joining the European Union in 1995, Finland has embraced more strongly the cultural ties with its Baltic neighbors and its central European partners. Its sense of isolation has eroded and now the Baltic is viewed more as a bridge than an obstacle.

Red-painted barns, wooden villages, and farms nestle near the indented coast to the east and west of Helsinki. Rolling, fertile farmland yielding lush crops of grain and cereals fills the woodland clearings, the reflections of red-brick mills and foundries are mirrored in lakes or fragmented in gentle rapids, and stone churches dominate the villages.

HANKO
Boulders perch incongruously on the sloping rock (facing page),
deposited by the retreating sheets of the Ice Age. Though frozen
solid in winter, the shallow bays and inlets on the southern coast
form natural swimming pools in mild summers (below).

HANKO

The town is blessed with many well-preserved wooden villas (facing page: top and bottom left), several of which operate as splendid summer guesthouses. There is also an almost childlike, dreamy quality to their towers (above) and seaside locations; sandy beaches and rocky shelves—with some inventive stone furniture (facing page: bottom right)—are excitingly close. Following double page: an isolated bathing hut occupies a sheltered beach.

The scattered archipelagos—a maze of pine-draped outcrops—crack the coastline all along the southern rim of the country down to the port of Hanko, with its elegant wooden villas and open sea views. For as long as the sea is free from ice, fishing boats plough silver furrows past cliffs of granite. The southern coast is also home to Swedish-speaking communities, this being the nation's second official language. Their cultural strongholds remain, for example, in the town of Porvoo (Borgå in Swedish), with its wooden old town spilling down to the rust-colored boathouses by the river, and Tammisaari (Ekenäs), with its yachting marina and waterside timber village.

Further to the east, towards the Russian border, the forest seems to grow a little wilder and the Swedish place names disappear. Here begins Karelia, a region divided by the Soviets after World War II and which retains a genuine frontier feel. Some 200,000 Finns moved out of the Soviet zone of Karelia at the end of the war; the survivors and their relatives regard the conceded area to the east of the border with wistful nostalgia. Karelia was also the inspiration for the Finnish national epic, *The Kalevala*, a saga of legends and myths collected by Elias Lönnrot in the nineteenth century, which remains a potent source of national imagery and sentiment. The art of Akseli Gallen-Kallela, a totem of aspiration for independence from Russian rule at the end of the nineteenth century, uses vivid motifs from this epic—witness the swirling fresco in Helsinki's National Museum—while the National Romantic decorations adorning the exterior of the same building are allusions to *The Kalevala's* Karelian imagery.

The lush forests of Karelia here cling to the shores of fabulous Saimaa, the essence of Finnish lakeland. Though commonly referred to as a single lake, Saimaa is actually a system, with a total shoreline running for some 9,300 miles (15,000 km) and studded with around 14,000 islands. Saimaa is a remnant of retreating glaciers; an isolated, elevated basin linking the town of Lappeenranta, near the border in the south, with Savonlinna (whose magnificent castle is the venue for an annual opera festival) and Joensuu in northern Karelia. Other lakeland

PORVOO

*Regarded by many as Finland's most picturesque town,
Porvoo is a favorite destination for excursions from Helsinki,
and is less than an hour's drive or a leisurely coastal cruise
from the capital. The houses of the old wooden town (far left
and right) cling to a slope leading down to the Porvoo river and
the town remains a thriving community, traditionally
inspirational for artists and writers. The Town Hall in the
cobbled square is now the town museum (left).*

towns in the east are Kuopio, a port for summer lake steamer traffic at the heart of the Savo province, and Kajaani. This hinterland is sprinkled with typically neat and quiet Finnish communities, unspectacular but pleasant, where grids of unassuming modern blocks, usually centered on a market square, have replaced most of the traditional wooden milieus—some destroyed by accidental fire, others by the commercial expediencies of development.

Further north, the lakes become smaller and more scattered, and the land grows more contoured towards the Arctic Circle. Ruka, near the town of Kuusamo, is the first winter sports resort; the fells of Lapland begin to swoop above the tree line and the rivers tumble into dramatic gorges. The Arctic Circle itself runs through the town of Rovaniemi, the provincial capital of Finnish Lapland, rebuilt according to plans by architect Alvar Aalto after its destruction at the hands of the retreating German army. Much of Finland's forest and countryside, though seemingly wild and desolate, is managed and farmed by the country's big paper companies.

North of Rovaniemi, however, Finland ascends to Europe's final genuine wilderness, where the windswept moors and mountains of the far northwestern arm rise up then spill down into the fjords of Norway. Finland's other Nordic neighbor, Sweden, lies across the Muonio and Tornio rivers. This is the home of the Sámi, the indigenous Lapps, and the road signs bear the place names in their language. It is also the home of the reindeer, farmed by the Sámi and more frequently sighted on some desolate highways than cars or people. This is one of Europe's most sparsely populated areas.

Moving south again, we come to the broad agricultural plains of Ostrobothnia and the towns of Oulu, Kokkola, Pietarsaari, Vaasa, Pori, and Rauma, strung along the coast of the Gulf of Bothnia. Pockets of wooden houses remain here, including the UNESCO-protected quarter of Rauma, and they provide a rustic antidote to the tidy grids of the predominant modern townscape. Further inland, the lakes accumulate again around the city of Tampere with its red-brick mills and picturesque wooden suburbs clinging to the steep glacial ridges. Hämeenlinna, the birthplace of Sibelius, boasts another fine lakeside castle.

Lastly, there is Finland's southwestern extremity, where thousands of islands appear to drift away from the mainland, like floes of ice from a glacier. The delightful Åland archipelago, whose capital Maarianhamina (Mariehamn in Swedish) is a traditional home to shipping magnates and sailors, is inhabited almost entirely by Swedish-speakers and shelters halfway between Finland and Sweden. On the mainland lies the port and old Finnish capital of Turku, divided by the tree-lined river Aura and

PORVOO

*Porvoo, founded under the Swedish
name of Borgå (meaning "castle river")
on the river of the same name (left),
acquired parish status in the thirteenth
century. Much of the attraction of the
wooden houses is derived from their
rustic simplicity, while sloping lanes
that wind down from the hilltop church
to the red riverside warehouses underline
the town's unique character.*

home to a Swedish speaking university and a towering fifteenth-century cathedral. From the capital of the past, the circuit heads back to Helsinki, the capital of the present.

The variations in the landscape are sufficient for the lie of the land in each region to influence and bias the mood and outlook of its inhabitants. In turn, these find expression in the local variations in the Finnish language. Sunlight reflecting on the Saimaa water shimmers through the quirky dialect of Savo; the people of Tampere and the rest of Häme have a distinctive slang. Local characteristics also belie the perceived uniformity of the Finnish persona. While the Finns are by no means the most outwardly expressive of European nations, neither are they as universally reserved and silent as their stereotype would have it. A Finnish dinner table may be as noisy—sometimes noisier—than any in Italy or France. The stereotype presents a lone and sulky figure, but the Finns are more gregarious than is often supposed. Resonating within its linguistic and geographical context, Finnish humor may sometimes be dark and dry to the outsider. Yet the successful and popular expression of such humor in the quintessentially Finnish cinema of the Kaurismäki brothers, Aki and Mika, proves it can transcend such a context.

Language, more than any other single factor, is what distinguishes the Finns, setting them apart from the rest of the Nordic nations, whose tongues are all quite closely related to one another. Finnish thrives and evolves, even though Swedish is the first language of about 6 percent of Finns. Although it belongs to the same Finno-Ugric linguistic family as Hungarian, the closest relation to Finnish is Estonian, spoken in its homeland to the south across the Gulf of Finland. Proficiency at other languages, particularly English, is both highly developed and necessary, meaning that the long vowels, sharp syllables, and elaborate grammar of Finnish erect no barrier to trade or cultural exchange. Yet the language, colored and molded as it is by loaned vocabulary from other tongues, provides a kind of ethnic refuge—an indomitable last cultural stand for the Finnish personality.

Lying on Finland's west coast, Old Rauma—one of Finland's six remaining medieval towns and listed by UNESCO—is an archetypal Scandinavian wooden urban milieu, and has survived the ravages of time, war, and fire remarkably well. Although records of Old Rauma date back to the fifteenth century, much of what remains was built in the eighteenth century. The buildings are clustered closely together and their roughly uniform height contributes to their agreeably harmonious effect. Window details (facing page: bottom center and right), street furniture such as a restored water pump (facing page: bottom left), and doorways (above and facing page: top) demonstrate the demands placed on the carpenters' skills.

A SEASONAL EBB AND FLOW

While Finland has made a conscious decision to be more closely identified, culturally and politically, with western and southern Europe, the influence it cannot choose to change, of course, is its climate. There are two primary shades to the Finnish landscape: the green of summer and the white of winter, and the moods of its people shift accordingly. The depths of introspective winter are best suited to mental activity, the erection of barriers in the mind against the elements. Yet winter does not arrive overnight with a single nationwide snowfall. The fall and its brash display of hues known as *ruska* linger in the south, but may be over within a week or two in the north. Lichens are transformed to vivid, rusty reds and oranges, the birch and maple glow with color, Virginia creeper flares across the sides of buildings, and scarlet berries hang heavy on the rowan trees. The first frosts of Lapland quickly follow this brilliant protest of nature against its own enforced hibernation, while in the south, Baltic storms lash the coasts. Christmas is usually white in the Arctic zones; in the south the permanent snow cover can take a little longer to accumulate.

Once winter has taken grip, the country is tucked up in a blanket of white. Ice thickens around the Baltic shores, reflecting a blinding glare, and the sea steams like soup where the icebreakers crush open the shipping lanes. Lapland becomes a playground for winter holidaymakers from the southern cities, for cross-country and alpine skiers. At Rovaniemi, aircraft crammed with Santa-seeking tourists arrive from all over Europe; they step into the snow-stifled landscape with the excitement of aliens alighting onto a new planet.

The exotica of winter provide the local population with all manner of revenue-raising enterprises, from the Santa Claus Post Office at the Arctic Circle to reindeer and snowmobile safaris through the tundra and golf competitions on the frozen lakes. Overhead, the benevolent, magical force of the Northern Lights flickers and flutters, a spectacular backdrop to the drama of the pristine fells. Visitors from Japan huddle like penguins on the frozen lakesides and hotel rooftops to witness the show.

RAUMA

The backstreets and courtyards of Old Rauma (facing page and right) reveal a more rustic but no less charming character than the finer, more detailed street façades. They also offer a glimpse of a somewhat crowded lifestyle, where the notion of privacy was alien and the scale and sophistication of the dwelling was a clear reflection of the occupant's wealth.

LAKELAND SAUNA

The view from the sauna at the House of Silence summer home in eastern Finland looks out across classic Finnish Lakeland scenery, drawing the elements of the natural environment into the sauna chamber and treating the bather to the calming light of the southern horizon (following double page).

Back in Helsinki and the other towns and cities, the population braces itself against the weather. The sun lurks close to the horizon in the south, while in the north it stays pinned beneath the horizon. This is the time for getting projects done, for planning and completing assignments, for keeping the weather at bay. Spring is slow to arrive, and a sense of impatience precedes the gradual thaw in Helsinki and the south. The flowers and foliage of central Europe are already well advanced before they appear in Finland, but spring makes up for lost time once it arrives, gathering pace in an explosion of growth. The May Day—*Vappu*—holiday remains a significant socialist festival, but is anticipated more for the celebratory license it affords. Students cavort in fountains, champagne is swigged from bottles, and there is universal relief at the progress of the annual cycle and the approach of summer, with its long, green, energetic, light-filled days.

The art of living in Finland is the art of submitting to these extremes, of shaping routines and lifestyles to the ebb and flow of the seasons. Finland is, of course, no stranger to seasonal transitions, yet they demand particular adjustments here. The awareness of light, including the inventiveness required to maximize its limited availability at one extreme and the immersion in its abundance at the other, is central to existence here. Because of the scarcity of direct light during the winter months,

Finland's artists and architects treasure it uniquely at any time of the year as an element of the environment as a whole. The light of summer, never-ending at the Arctic zenith and dimming after midnight to semi dusk in the south, enchants and dislocates, while the reflected, eerie blue of the *kaamos*, when the sun struggles to rise above the horizon, has its own magical quality.

It is no coincidence that many of Helsinki's most assertive monuments—the National Opera House, the Finlandia Hall, and the Olympic Stadium—are an uncomplicated, reflective white. An entire phase of the career of Alvar Aalto, the designer of Finlandia, was known as his "white period," and his designs were keenly aware of the relationship between the shifting light and the environment. His use of natural light from roof skylights is a clear statement of an awareness inherited by more contemporary architects, including Juhani Pallasmaa, who has taken account not only of the light, but also of the sounds and other sensations mirrored in the Finnish natural environment. Reima Pietilä lived just long enough to see his last creation—the official residence of the president of Finland at Mäntyniemi in Helsinki—completed in 1993; this is also an essay of sympathy with the surroundings, with trees and granite boulders reflected in the broad, low windows.

SUOMENLINNA
Having alighted from the ferry arriving from Helsinki's main
Market Square, visitors to the eighteenth-century island fortress
of Suomenlinna pass through the archway (left, bottom)
in the quayside barracks. The fortress, guarding the entrance
to the capital's South Harbor and the city's most historic
and beautiful single attraction at any time of the year,
remains the permanent home to a small community residing
in apartment blocks (left, top), as well as the temporary
residence of sailors from the naval academy.
The imposing King's Gate with its King's Steps and drawbridge
(facing page) was constructed in 1753–1754 and was intended
as a ceremonial entrance to the fortress complex; its name
refers to King Adolf Fredrik of Sweden, the founder
of the fortress. Suomenlinna means "fortress of Finland"
in Finnish: its construction began at a time when Finland
was part of Sweden, but was eventually occupied
by the Russians whom it was designed to repel.
(Suomenlinna is described on page 143).

A similar empathy echoes in the music of Sibelius, whose meditative tone poems are suggestive of the moods of shifting light. Unsurprisingly, it also appears in pictorial art, from traditional landscape portrayals to more abstract works. The entire catalog of Finnish designers, from the glassware of Tapio Wirkkala to the textile designs of Marimekko, pays homage to the muse of the natural environment.

Almost every strand of Finnish creativity, from its melancholy poetry and music to its sculpture and architecture, can be traced to this awareness of the landscape and the seasonal shifts in mood, either conscious or subliminal. Finland takes its cue from Nordic culture and tradition, from the comforts of the Scandinavian instincts for social welfare and sound infrastructure, and a similar attachment to the environment can be seen in its neighbors, Sweden and Norway. Finland has opted for a western, European future, yet Finnish identity and roots are encoded in a distinct Finno-Ugric language and psychology, whose threads lead to an eastern heritage and a meditative connection with the forests, lakes, and immeasurable horizon.

LAPLAND

Finland's only true mountains are in the far north, above the Arctic Circle, in Lapland (left). Here, the scenery rises to windswept fells above the tree line, and in many areas reindeer outnumber people. In winter, the fells are covered with a thick carpet of snow, providing an extensive and exciting setting for winter sports of all descriptions.

HELSINKI—A CITY OF THE SEA

A broad circular sweep of Finland reveals gradual changes in the landscape and its inhabitants. Yet the drama of the landscape resides in its sheer scale rather than its variety. Peer from the window of an aircraft approaching Helsinki on a clear day and that scale cannot fail to impress. Approaching Finland from the air is like flying into a dreamy idyll; not so much the land that time forgot as the land that forgot time.

At first sight, the subtleties and variety of the landscape are completely unapparent. The country sprawls to the north in what appears to be a vast, continuous forest, broken only by the sheen of glittering lakes and rivers. To the east, the patchwork continues—the European edge of an expanse that blends into the taiga of Siberia, crossing the Urals and stretching to the Pacific seaboard. If you squint a little, the clusters of urban settlements, blend into this illusion of eternal wilderness, and you can see the landscape as if human eyes had never witnessed it before. Twist your head to the south—the fragmented coastline, sprinkled with countless islands, seems similarly unpopulated.

As becomes clear as you descend towards Helsinki, this seeming wilderness is in fact punctuated by an especially modern civilization. Here thrives a culture carved from the forest and weathered by the harshest extremes of European climate, close to its roots in the simplicity of nature, yet at the very cusp of technological progress. As your plane approaches the airport, you make out the broad, uncluttered highways, sweeping through the woodlands. The settlements march in an orderly and gradually depleted progression away from the city, yet the impression is welcoming rather than brisk and alienating.

Few capital cities exude such a sense of newness, and this first impression as you approach is oddly emphasized by the comforting lushness of its rural environs. The Nuuksio National Park, for example, one of the most compact of the many scattered through the country,

HELSINKI
The Uspensky Orthodox Cathedral (above) towers over red brick warehouses on the Katajanokka promontory, providing a visual and cultural contrast with the nearby Lutheran Cathedral, originally the Church of St. Nicholas (facing page: bottom). The Lutheran Cathedral was the centerpiece of the administrative facility planned for the newly appointed capital of the Grand Duchy of Finland in the first half of the nineteenth century, designed by Carl Ludvig Engel (1778–1840). Both cathedrals are clearly visible from the South Harbor, from which sailing boats set off for summer voyages towards the outer skerries of the coastal archipelago (facing page: top).

HELSINKI

The neoclassical buildings of Helsinki's South Harbor waterfront and Market Square (right) include the City Hall and the Swedish Embassy and are dominated by the gleaming white Lutheran Cathedral. The striking Sibelius Monument (below) by Eila Hiltunen, in the Sibelius park, includes a bust of the great Finnish composer.

is just an hour's drive from the center of the capital, and provides a microcosm of the broader themes of Finnish landscape, of forest, rock, and water. Helsinki's Central Park is a swathe of forest stretching its tendrils through the suburbs of the city, rather than a park in the usual ordered sense.

Moving from the air to the land, you appreciate the rate and extent of urban expansion. A battalion of cranes besieges each section of the city in turn, rotating continuously in a process of obsessive renewal. Finland's feverish enthusiasm for keeping the infrastructure of its capital in good condition is an inescapable manifestation of its affluence. Roads are resurfaced, cavernous shopping malls annexed, and houses repainted and renovated with extraordinary regularity. Helsinki experienced the fastest growth of any capital in Europe during part of the 1990s. Although this has slowed in the capital proper, it continues in the neighboring cities of Vantaa and Espoo.

The fact that Vantaa and Espoo, two collections of mostly unlinked suburbs, are referred to and categorized officially as cities reveals something of the Finnish approach to urban life. The Greater Helsinki Area, with its million or so inhabitants, sits on the southern tip of a country that extends for well over six hundred miles (1,000 km) to the north. The economic pull of the capital region has uprooted populations from all over the country, replanting them in the south, and turning them overnight into urbanites. Outside the capital area, no town or city is home to more than two or three hundred thousand people. A fifth of the country's inhabitants are within the magnetic pull of its biggest conurbation.

To understand the pleasures and rigors of life in Finland, it is also necessary to understand this transitional process, still in progress, whereby the Finns bring their rural psychology to the urban experience. The Finn is armed with the latest technology, from the state-of-the-art, designed-in-Finland Nokia phone to the fastest and most efficient remote

PARLIAMENT ANNEX AND NOKIA HOUSE
Nokia House, the main offices of the Finnish telecommunications giant (above), is located in Espoo just to the west of Helsinki. The futuristic palace of steel and glass, designed by Pekka Helin and Tuomo Siitonen, is an aptly high-tech statement, but was conceived with the intention of nurturing creative, human interaction. Pekka Helin was also in charge of the team that designed the new annex to the Finnish parliament (facing page), in which wooden interiors are used to soften the glass and steel.

The arriving and departing Stockholm ferries in Helsinki's South
Harbor (right) crush the ice and leave a swirling, steaming wake
of icy water, shrouding in dramatic, tinted mist the NJK yacht
club building and Klippan restaurant on their respective islands.

payment methods. Sometimes it can be difficult for the outsider to reconcile the fervent devotion to technology with the equal dedication to the rural.

In Helsinki itself it is the freshness of the sea that dominates, rather than the scents of the forest. The sea is always close and the city's harbors infiltrate its very heart. Huge ferries—the biggest car ferries in the world—edge away from the South Harbor daily on their voyages to Stockholm, as if whole quarters of Helsinki were breaking away into the water. In October, the same harbor hosts a Herring Fair, where small vessels from the archipelagos line up along the quay by the Market Square to sell their wares. The beaches and restaurants on the offshore islands are the city's summer leisure haunts, while the sea itself, often covered by thick ice in winter, extends into a supplementary parkland, frequented by strollers, kite-flyers, ice fishermen, and skiers. Many of Helsinki's attractions are on islands too: the Open Air Museum of Seurasaari, the zoo, and the magnificently romantic, windswept island fortress of Suomenlinna.

Whole suburbs have been constructed on land reclaimed from the sea. The district of Ruoholahti to the west of the center, for example, has changed from a crumbling shoreside wasteland to a gleaming procession of glass and painted steel of apartment blocks and office complexes. Closer to the center, modern showpieces overshadow the more sedate and older quarters. The quirky, rustic details of Jugendstil doors and windows in the areas of Katajanokka and Kruunuhaka, for instance, are more endearing but less striking than the curved tube of Steven Holl's Kiasma, the Museum of Contemporary Art, and its glass cube of a neighbor, the Sanoma House.

Further along the inlet of the Töölö bay, Alvar Aalto's showpiece Finlandia Hall follows the lie of the land, its theme of shining white

HELSINKI

*Finland's National Opera moved from the Alexander Theater
(facing page: bottom center), built in 1879 when Finland was
still a Russian Grand Duchy, to a National Opera House (above),
one of the city's most striking examples of new public architecture
designed by Eero Hyvämäki, Jukka Karhunen, and Risto
Parkkinen, in 1993. Helsinki's rich architectural catalog also
embraces the villa style of the NJK yacht club house (facing
page: top) and the quirky National Romantic details of the stone
bear guarding the entrance of the National Museum (facing
page: bottom left), as well as the "guardians" of the main
Railway Station (facing page: bottom right).*

continued further around the bay at the National Opera House and again at the Olympic Stadium with its landmark viewing-tower. Meanwhile, other developments proceed apace: the Kamppi Center, with its underground bus station, apartments and shops, was the biggest single construction project ever undertaken in Finland; a new music center is planned that may add to the cluster of new buildings near Kiasma, an antidote to the stern columns of the Parliament House across the main thoroughfare of Mannerheimintie.

For those who approach from the sea—as many visitors do—by ferry from Stockholm and central Europe or by Baltic cruise liner, Helsinki reveals itself as hugging a low profile. Few landmarks break a regular skyline, with the exception of a church spire here, a chimney there. In empathy with the sensible humility of its people, this is not a city that overstates itself in high-rise projects. Rather, there is something refreshingly stolid about its outline. Helsinki knows its place and makes the most of it.

Recently, this has meant submitting to the influences from across the Baltic, as well as absorbing and exuding some of the cosmopolitan atmospheres of central Europe. On a warm summer day, the tree-lined Esplanade running down to the harbor, with its determined shoppers and tables spilling out onto the wide pavements from the proliferating cafés and restaurants, is reminiscent of the Barcelona *Ramblas* or some busy Paris boulevard. The ever-multiplying chorus of languages of different visitors from Russia, Estonia, Sweden, Italy, France, and Britain adds an international resonance. Helsinki, so long in the shadow of its Nordic counterparts of Stockholm and Copenhagen to the west and once so cautious of Russia to the east, has the air of a city that has come of age.

2

INTERIORS

On the one hand, submission to the wiles of Finland's winter weather is inevitable; on the other, the Finns have developed a lifestyle that maintains comfort in their homes and other buildings. The no-nonsense Finn has little time for superfluous luxury or opulence, and while taste and elegance are rarely sacrificed, structural security and practicality are the essence of life in this country. Houses and shops are invariably well heated in winter; it may be minus twenty degrees Celsius (-4°F) outside but it will always be more than plus twenty (68°F) indoors. Finnish towns and cities organize their services well, and roads are cleared of snow almost as quickly as it falls. Cozy cabins and fine hotels are perched across the fells of the most remote northern areas, offering the most civilized refuge from the wildest Arctic elements.

Winter is a fact of Finnish life, but summer is more of a celebration here than a season. Log cabins, cottages, and saunas are dotted around the shores of Finland's thousands of lakes and inlets—an idyllic summer setting. Although modern Finns are a well-traveled species, nothing suits them better than to decamp from town or city to a second home in the country or by the lakeside in Finland itself, or to cruise at leisure around

LAPILA MANOR
Page 52: The salon in the manor at Lapila in southwestern Finland retains elements of its original eighteenth-century classical Swedish style.

GUESTHOUSE
The veranda of a summer guesthouse designed by Pekka Helin (left) shows the more intimate side of an architect better known for large-scale public structures.

A SENSE OF INTIMACY
A gazebo on a rocky outcrop above Lake Kallavesi in eastern Finland (facing page: bottom center), built to the designs of Juhani Pallasmaa, was conceived as a "secluded place for family meals, celebrations, and meditation in the middle of wild nature," where the interior and surrounding landscape are harmoniously united. It was first erected next to another lake as part of a summer exhibition in 2002, and lifted in completed form into its present location by a large crane. Facing page: The wooden herb mortar (top) by Tuuli Autio looks at home in this forested setting, as do the glasses by Modisia's Jussi Mäkelä, the classic glass candle holders from Iittala by Annaleena Hakatie, and the birch fruit bowl (bottom left and right) by Petri Vainio from Artek's collection. Juha Leiviskä's Pendant lamp sheds an intimate light over Vainio's bowl, glasses and bowls from Iittala's Teema range by Kaj Franck, and an oak vase (bottom left and right).

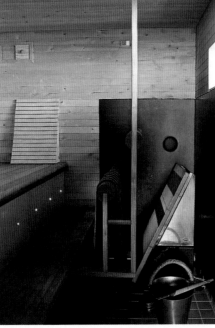

THE SAUNA
*The sauna is an enduring aspect of Finnish culture,
and the fundamental elements of the steam chamber have not
altered much from the basic traditional log structure (far left)
to more recent modern versions (left).*

PROFESSOR NIELS RAÏHA'S HOUSE
*This log cabin, built in 1880, is primarily a vacation home on the
island of Villinge in the archipelago six miles (10 km) east of
Helsinki. Family portraits adorn the entrance to the veranda,
which is furnished with Gustavian wooden chairs (facing page).*

the coastal islands. Here is the first of many paradoxes with which the Finns—so uncomplicated on first encounter—confuse their guests: their love of civilization, of systems, of things that *work,* is equaled only by their instinctive, almost pagan appreciation of their natural environment. Accordingly, Finnish sophistication, in terms of lifestyle, culture, and manners, is without pretentiousness and is scornful of snobbery.

The sauna ritual is in keeping with this character. The sauna—with the exception of Nokia, the word is the only item of Finnish vocabulary to have entered global parlance—has retained its appeal and popularity in parallel to the glitzier technological distractions of the modern world. Although the once common public sauna is a rare facility these days, most apartment blocks and hotels in the towns and cities, as well as many individual residences, swimming pools, and sports centers, are equipped with at least one sauna. The electrically heated variety is by necessity most common in these circumstances, though still a compromise on the authentic sauna: a quaint but simple wooden chamber heated by a wood-burning stove and located close to water.

Sauna bathing is a link to the rustic roots of the Finnish character and an element of cultural heritage. The sauna was the functional center of a rural family's routine: a place to congregate, to wash, and even to give birth. Today, it is viewed as a therapeutic and essential component of any leisure-time sojourn in a summer home. Sauna bathing is popular in winter, too: although the act of bathing in a hot and sooty hut before rolling in the snow or dipping in icy lake water seems eccentric to the visitor, the Finn will gleefully insist on the efficacy of such behavior.

Back in their modern, warmly insulated urban homes, the Finns maximize the resources of precious light, so abundant in summer and—at least until the reflective snow accumulates—so scarce in the depths of winter. The apartment balcony or house porch and patio will ideally face south, and much use is made of white walls and fittings in the Finnish interior to amplify the ambient illumination. Older homes and manors exhibit a similar sensitivity to the availability of natural light, although the conscious and explicit application of such sensitivity in architectural art matured in the twentieth century with the emergence of Finnish architects such as Alvar Aalto and Juhani Pallasmaa. Yet even the most forward-looking, radical, and modernistic Finnish architects or interior designers pay homage to the particular qualities of the Finnish landscape —its rugged components of wood and rock, as well as the extremes of light and climate—as an influence on their work.

ALVAR AALTO'S VILLA MAIREA

Villa Mairea nestles in the forest on a hill above the industrial village of Noormarkku, close to the west coast city of Pori. The red wooden buildings clustered around the pools and rapids, the grand manor belonging to the Ahlström family, and the horses grazing in the meadows evoke a simple, pastoral idyll, amid which Mairea expresses an exceptional architectural sophistication.

The villa is concealed and isolated behind its screen of trees and, superficially at least, makes little reference in its outward modernity to the nineteenth-century industry of sawmills and hammer forges so well preserved in its neighboring buildings. At the same time, it is hard to imagine Villa Mairea in any other location.

Alvar Aalto designed the villa for Harry Gullichsen (1902–1954), the director of the Ahlström company that continues to own and operate in the estate, and his wife Maire (1907–1990), a member of the Ahlström family. Aalto's wife, Aino, is also credited with the interior design of the villa, which was constructed between 1937 and 1939. In terms of architectural significance as a private residence, with its relatively uncompromised demonstration of the architect's ideals and aspirations, Villa Mairea is on a par with the Fallingwater house in Pennsylvania by Frank Lloyd Wright and the Villa Savoye at Poissy by Le Corbusier.

The main entrance to the house, on the south side, leads the visitor under a sheltered, curved awning of wooden panels and into a hallway and reception area, separated from the open living space by a low white wall. A few steps to the left take the visitor up into this spacious living area, where the Gullichsens would welcome their guests and in which occasional music recitals were—and still are—staged.

VILLA MAIREA
The columns bound with rattan in the living space of Villa Mairea (left) are a device used to draw in the elements of nature from the nearby forest. The wall to the left is a screen added at the request of the owner, Harry Gullichsen, to preserve the privacy of the library on the other side. The 1920s glass-topped piano is by Danish designer Poul Henningsen.

VILLA MAIREA

The villa remains a fitting showcase for prototype 1930s Artek furniture and fittings (facing page), much of which are still in production today. The Artek style had a revolutionary effect on the art of design, celebrating a modest harmony in their combination of materials, colors, and simple forms—a blend that is triumphantly reflected in the complete and equally influential statement made by the villa. The living space spills out from the house into the crook of the building that encloses a yard, a swimming pool, and greenery that extends beyond stonewalls and wooden fences into the untamed forest (right, top and bottom).

Dozens of pine slats form a regular ceiling throughout the continuous, partition-free living rooms, also serving as a means of distributing the air ventilation. Although the space is open, it is divided into two very different types of interior, distinguished by the floor materials. Finnish red slate is used in the north-facing area, with white beech employed as a surface in the south-facing corner.

Alvar and Aino Aalto aimed for—and achieved—an easy contrast between the two spaces, with a more contemplative Nordic feel to the north, dominated by a massive roaring fireplace, and an airier, more feminine, and Asian ambience in the southern section, with its 1920s glass-topped piano by Danish designer Poul Henningsen. This Asian theme is also pursued in the adjacent Japanese-style flower room, filled with wicker furniture, shelves of plants that thrive with a health that is startling for the northern corner of a Nordic house, and a watering bath. The stone floor continues through a door directly onto the terrace, towards the forest.

A book-lined library—a private area isolated by an irregular partition—completes the south side of the ground floor plan. In Aalto's original plan, the library was open, in line with his principle of visual communication between different parts of the house and providing a contact with the rest of the living area, but Harry Gullichsen requested that it be closed off to ensure the privacy of an office environment. Aalto met the request by using alternate panels of wood and glass, a combination that provides attractive decorative effects when the evening winter sun sprawls through the windows.

The long dining room, staff dining space, kitchen, and pantry occupy the eastern "foot" of the "L" plan, with serving doors leading to the

VILLA MAIREA

The house is built in an "L" formation, with the "back"
of the L facing south and collecting the surprising amount
of light that filters through the woods (left). A stone-paved
terrace extends along the inner rim of the house (below), and
there is a sense of private, secluded calm, evocative of the
luxurious traditional villas of Italy.

main table, and a fireplace at the far, northern end. This fireplace is duplicated on the outside of the building, providing an pleasant focus for outdoor summer gatherings on the shaded terrace or refreshments after swimming and bathing in the sauna on its northern side. The sauna roof and that of the eastern wing are covered with thick turf, a traditional Finnish idiom that is surprisingly in keeping with the Asian and Renaissance villa elements.

Taking the staircase to the first floor, the visitor passes the wooden columns, wound in places with rattan—an effect that deliberately brings to mind the forest that is visible through the windows, drawing the soothing features of nature into the interior. At the top of the stairs, one is immediately struck by the familiar intimacy of the style, compared with the more public expansiveness of the ground floor.

Maire Gullichsen was a gifted artist in her own right. The studio, with its gallery and wide windows, provided a refuge in which she could pursue her artistic endeavors. One of the originally intended functions of the house was to showcase Maire's own impressive collection; original works from this collection, mainly representing European Modernism, still adorn the walls.

The children's bedrooms on the same floor, with their bright yellow floors and climbing frames, were the result of consideration for what an active child's space ought to include, setting an example for the kindergartens of the twenty-first century. This attention to design detail is repeated in the minutiae of the door handles, stair structures, and plywood birch cupboards in the kitchens. It was also behind the founding in 1935 of the Artek design company by Alvar and Aino in collaboration with Maire and art historian Nils-Gustav Hahl—a pivotal event in the evolution of Finnish design.

VILLA MAIREA
The open space of the northern side of the main living area (right) focuses on a giant fireplace, while a wooden staircase leads up to the more intimate privacy of the family bedrooms and Maire Gullichsen's studio.

HEIKKI SIRÉN'S ARCHIPELAGO
"SEA CHAPEL": SIMPLICITY AND MEDITATION

In distant silhouette, viewed from an approaching boat, the "Sea Chapel" on the private island belonging to the Sirén family appears as an anomalous block: geometrical perfection set in the context of natural, wild asymmetry. Yet the structure, built from pine and glass on a wind-blown rocky platform exposed to the open Baltic, seems rooted in the rock as naturally and firmly as any of the stunted trees that hug the island behind it.

This is not a chapel in any accepted sense. Unlike the celebrated Lutheran chapel at Otaniemi in Espoo on the mainland whose architect, Heikki Sirén, it shares, it contains no religious symbols or paraphernalia. It is ideal, however, for its intended function of quiet and private meditation. A sense of privacy prevails, despite the fact that the walls of the structure are made of glass panels that reach from floor to ceiling, allowing images of the surrounding nature to come flooding in. The sturdy pine beams, floor, and roof that complete this minimalist perfection contrast with the fragility of the glass, and the occupant feels secure and protected from the often-frenzied elements.

The chapel was built on the island of Lingonsö in the Barösund archipelago, to the west of Helsinki off the southwest coast along the Gulf of Finland, in 1969. The original idea, according to Jukka Sirén—Heikki's son and himself an architect—was to build a gazebo-type structure to complement the family's vacation homes on the other side of the large island. The result came to be referred to as the "Sea Chapel," because its design and location make it the perfect retreat for meditation and contemplation.

"It's a wonderful place to sit when the waves and storm are raging, while one sits in silence inside," says Jukka. "My family has been in the archipelago since 1936 when my grandfather (J.S. Sirén, who designed

SEA CHAPEL
The landscape of the southern Finnish archipelago, which is the setting for Heikki Sirén's "Sea Chapel," is characterized by rugged outcrops of granite (left), often streaked with vivid veins of color and molded by centuries of storms.

SEA CHAPEL
*The design of the Sea Chapel (preceding double page) is ingeniously
simple and sturdy, introducing a geometrical component that is
remarkably at home in a completely asymmetrical landscape.
The wooden pillars and glass walls (facing page) provide the
occupant with a panoramic and almost tangible
view of the archipelago landscape (right).*

Helsinki's domineering Parliament House) built on another island in
the same area. The island homes are designed for use in the summertime, and it was the wish of my brother, who is a part-owner, to construct
something on the southern side of the same island where one can see
only the horizon."

The striking simplicity of the resulting structure is reminiscent of a
kind of oriental minimalism, but Jukka prefers to make a comparison
with the work of Mies van der Rohe. "There is, of course, something
very basic in the form of architecture where you have only column and
beam. It was my father's aim to create a kind of shelter with the simplest
structural means."

Glass walls surround the occupant, and the bench seating is in a
recessed pit so that one can sit at a lower level and look towards the horizon from that visual perspective. There is storage space for pillows under
the simple sofa mattresses, but otherwise the space is uncluttered with
furniture or fittings. There is no heating in the chapel, although the
overnight visitor is greeted with morning warmth and can open the glass
doors to angles of 180 degrees and continue sleeping.

"My father's career is characterized by very strong simplicity," says
Jukka. "In the Sea Chapel, it would be hard to make things any simpler,
but the visible structural detail is in fact very ingenious."

Jukka sees this simplicity as an element of the Finnish approach to
design and architecture. "Finnish style is a state of mind, a mental ques-
tion," he muses. "There are of course many kinds of Finnish architect,
but at one extreme is a modesty and simplicity combined with craftsmanship, a tendency to work out solutions for as long as it takes to find
harmony between the content, the structure, and the surroundings of a
building."

Jukka Sirén states his preference for disciplined architecture, which
is not unusual for a nation that has had to reconstruct itself after the
ferocity of world war. "Finnish design and architecture have grown from
minimalism," he says. "It's quite natural here. People have always had
to work on projects in ways that extract maximum output from minimum
resources. After the war we had big problems with shortages of steel and
concrete and even wood. Now we live in a world where there is too much
of everything. Nonetheless, there will always be people who appreciate
minimalism."

He gestures through the window of his Helsinki studio that looks out
across the beautiful wooded islands of the archipelago, adding: "And
when you have a natural environment like ours, you don't need rococo
or other stylistic complications."

AN ESSAY ON LIGHT AT THE VILLA FURUHOLM, RUISSALO ISLAND

The dozens of handsome, wooden villas sheltered in lush woodlands on the island of Ruissalo close to the city of Turku are an elegant legacy of the bourgeois Swedish villa culture that came to prominence in the early nineteenth century. They are a sign of the persistence of Swedish cultural influence in Finland, even after the transfer of the country's imperial rule from Swedish to Russian hands in 1809. Indeed, Swedish influence remains, not least in the prominence of the Swedish language in this region. Many of the villas are beautifully preserved and offer a languid throwback to a bygone age.

The impetus for the construction of the villas came with a serious fire in the city of Turku that destroyed many of the finest bourgeois houses. Attention was drawn to Ruissalo, which today is connected to the southwest suburb of the city by a short bridge. It was claimed as the sixteenth-century hunting reserve of Duke Johan, and its gently rolling landscape has enjoyed an unusual abundance of lush oaks and other deciduous vegetation ever since. In 1845 the Imperial Senate gave permission for the building of forty-nine villas, forty-six of which on the main island and the remaining three on the smaller adjacent island of Iso-Pukki.

The fabulous private villa of Furuholm is one of the three licensed residences on Iso-Pukki and is reached by boat from a small marina on Ruissalo's southern shore. Now owned and occupied every summer by local author and historian Marjo Brunow-Ruola and her husband Pekka Ruola, the house still contains its original nineteenth-century furniture and is lovingly maintained in the spirit of its heyday. Marjo is so immersed in the period that she can be seen from passing boats attired in authentic costume on summer mornings, just as the original villa owners' wives might have been a century and a half before. "I love everything about the period," she says. "I am like a ghost on those summer mornings."

Villa Furuholm was planned as a leisure home for the Wilén family, whose printing and publishing business still thrives in Turku. Gustaf Wilhelm Wilén and his wife, Augusta, played an influential role in the design of the villa, playing close attention to the details of how the dreamy, extended summer light would penetrate its rooms and corners. The house was constructed on stone foundations as a simple Empire-style refuge by Augusta's father in 1845, and then extended by architect Stephan Michailow with Neo-Renaissance elements under the directions of Gustaf Wilhelm.

VILLA FURUHOLM

Sunlight flickers through the trees and dances on the water close to the Villa Furuholm (left). Refreshments are served on a porch to welcome guests just off the boat from the mainland (below).

VILLA FURUHOLM

*The same items of Empire-style and neo-rococo furniture
have graced the salon of Villa Furuholm since it was
inhabited by the Wilén family in the mid-nineteenth century
(left, top and bottom). The present owners re-enact the leisurely,
idyllic summers in what has been maintained as an
extraordinary living museum (facing page).*

Marjo Brunow-Ruola has decided to reinstate the decorative Japanese-style tower, which was removed by previous owners on the dubious grounds of child safety.

In the nineteenth century as now, guests would be welcomed at the jetty and a flag was displayed in honor of their arrival. They would pause on the porch, which offers a view down to the forested landscape. Inside the house, Augusta's Empire-style furniture, with its gray and mustard yellow upholstery and lyre-backed chairs, still graces the salon on one side, while a contrasting suite of neo-rococo red chairs occupies the other. Marjo and Pekka have painstakingly preserved the period ambience with portraits of Czar Nicholas II and Alexandra Feodorovna and romantic landscapes, as well as a neo-rococo table bearing a basket for holding visiting cards and a collection of cards displayed in an album.

Throughout the house, Augusta's harmonious color scheme remains, expressed in gentle white relieved by light browns, yellow, and eggshell blue. The style was a deliberate and successful attempt to create an airy, sunny contrast to the heavier tones of city life. Light filters softly into the salon—the most important and central room—through the silk drapes across the three wide windows.

More treasures remain in the upstairs rooms, including the bedrooms once occupied by the Wiléns's daughters, Agda and Martha. Augusta's feminine touch is visible in the silk and basket handicrafts, and plants and flowers still flourish in the villa, as she intended.

THE HOUSE OF SILENCE:
IN TUNE WITH FINNISH NATURE

The House of Silence is the Finnish summer home par excellence. It takes all of the classic, timeless elements of the Finnish country vacation home and reworks them in a unique modern idiom. It contains all the comforts of the most modern home, while retaining a quiet reverence for its remote lakeside setting. It affords the luxury of inner silence referred to in its name, but engages all the other senses, including sight, smell, and—strange as it may seem—sound.

The house was built according to the designs of architect Juhani Pallasmaa on a wooded slope, strewn with granite rocks and boulders, leading down to a small lake—small by Finnish standards, that is—some nineteen miles (30 km) from the town of Kouvola in southeastern Finland. Pallasmaa drew up the designs in the 1990s to replace some lakeside buildings in southern Finland owned by his wife's family. Building restrictions, however, prevented him from putting these plans into practice for his family's holiday home. But later, a musician friend spied the drawings and asked Pallasmaa if he might adapt the plans for his own twenty-hectare plot of lakeside land.

A delighted Pallasmaa agreed, and the project proceeded almost exactly to its original design. The House of Silence is the name given to the main house, but just as important is the adjacent sauna and "spa," the two being brought a little closer together than had been envisaged in the original plans. Otherwise the aspect of the location—facing south across the lake and receiving the full sweep of the sun's daily progress through the trees—was perfect for what Juhani Pallasmaa had in mind.

Pallasmaa's musician friend and his wife, whose own main home is a discreet third of a mile (0.5 km) away, describe the House of a Silence

HOUSE OF SILENCE
The House of Silence (right) stretches along a wooded slope overlooking a Finnish lake, like a pair of open arms embracing the southern source of light. A stonewall and slatted fence enclose a terrace close to the entrance where summer barbecues are held. Architect Juhani Pallasmaa has taken the opportunity to reinterpret the traditional features of the Finnish holiday home in a unique and imaginative manner.

A HAVEN OF REST
*An outdoor Japanese bathtub (facing page) provides an
alternative to the sauna in an annex to the House of Silence,
offering a panoramic, restful view across the lake. In the main
house, guests may dine intimately at a table in a booth (right).*

as a "crazy dream that came true, and a happy coincidence." The desire for silence, in the sense of inner, meditative peace, was a priority for them, and they recognized the potential for achieving this in Pallasmaa's plans. The title, House of Silence, came as the project progressed, as it became clear that the quality of silence would, indeed, be dominant. The project was completed in 2002.

As one approaches from the track to the east, the house resembles the prow of one half of an elegant boat slicing through the forest—an impression that Pallasmaa confirms is deliberate. This design is to emphasize the length of the house, following the contour of the slope from east to west. The outer structure of tarred wood and tubular steel stands in harmonious reference to the surrounding forest. Low walls composed of granite stones and an extended arbor embrace the eastern end of the main house. This encloses a flat and sheltered forecourt, where barbecues and outdoor gatherings can take place, allowing visitors to inhale the scents of the forest and contemplate the soft brush of the wind in the trees. A little further down the slope, to the west, lie the sauna building and a flight of wooden steps leading down to the lake and jetty.

The exteriors are striking, but not at the expense of the setting. Nature remains the dominant force, and this sense of protection both by and from the elements is maintained as one enters. The wooden walls are stained a light, reflective shade, and the first impression is of restrained and tasteful modernity. The main room of the house is fronted by a wide, gentle curve and a panoramic series of windows opening out to the trees, the sky, and the sparkling lake.

This curved format, together with windows strategically placed at either end, allows the daylight to enter the house during all its daily phases, changing the mood of the interior according to its brightness, contrast, and volume. In the center of the curve, almost due south, is a fireplace shielded by glass at both front and rear, which means one can sit and gaze through the fire towards the swaying trees and down to the lake some fifty-five yards (50 m) away. Outside and behind the fireplace, rainwater is channeled from the roof along a hanging pole, while in the winter, the flames flicker against a backdrop of snow.

Again the combination of elements is calculated, as it is throughout the house. The ambience is made conducive to reflection and introspection by the curved sweep of the façade, as if the essences of nature were absorbed and benignly contained by the structure, with nature itself looking in on the occupant as much as the occupant gazing out at nature. As Pallasmaa himself has said: "The interplay of nature and

architecture has the capacity of silencing the internal nervous clatter caused by urban stress, and enables the dweller to recover the precious silence of his or her soul."

The owners have kept decoration in the house to a minimum, so there is no distraction from the opportunities provided by the sweeping view. The main house has two levels, with two bedrooms and a sheltered balcony on the top floor, opening onto a gallery that looks down on the main room and fireplace. The shoreline in all directions is unoccupied by other houses or settlements; apart from the picturesque view of a farm obtainable from the jetty, no other houses or buildings are visible from the House of Silence.

Down in the sauna building, with its back wall curved as a reversed reference to its larger neighbor, a long strip window offers bathers an unimpeded vista down to the shore and across the lake, through a narrow channel between two headlands, and beyond to the hazy horizon. A similar view awaits bathers indulging in the sunken Japanese bathtub outside the sauna. Small loudspeakers are inserted in the sauna chamber, so bathers have the option of added musical relaxation.

Pallasmaa has said that he regards the House of Silence as an heir to the tradition of Ainola, the erstwhile home of composer Jean Sibelius's family, designed by Lars Sonck and built in the early twentieth century on the shores of the Tuusulanjärvi, just north of Helsinki. Sibelius requested a view of the lake from his main windows, as well as a prominent fireplace. Clearly, these are not unusual features for a Finnish home, but the elevated position of Ainola above the lakeshore and the sense of quiet, inward-looking repose are repeated in Pallasmaa's work.

Just as clearly, the House of Silence draws on and benefits from the other aspects of lakeside life in Finland. No such home would be complete without a sauna, for example. The bounty of the forest is on its doorstep, with the forest floor carpeted in berries in late summer and mushrooms

HOUSE OF SILENCE
The architect Juhani Pallasmaa directs the visitor's gaze toward an infinite point between the two sides of a narrow passage in the lake.

SILENCE AND LIGHT

Inside the House of Silence, light infiltrates the house at every passage and angle, sometimes forcefully, sometimes gently (above). The broad curve of the wide, south-facing series of windows in the main living area (facing page: top) provides as much visual interest as any visitor could hope for, while the central fireplace focuses the gaze through the flames, across the mossy forest floor and towards the shore of the lake. Facing page: The stairs to the upper floor (bottom left) lead to the bedrooms (bottom right), while a quiet lounge nestles in the northeastern corner (bottom center). The cushions are made from paper yarn and are from the Woodnotes Cool collection.

in fall. The House of Silence is one more piece of evidence that the Finns' ties with the natural environment have survived the urbanization of Finnish society.

"The fact that the design was originally for my family made it more intimate," says Juhani Pallasmaa, who was born in 1936. "This was probably the best client I have ever had in terms of understanding my intentions. It also happened that the building was built by local craftsmen who had never built a curved wall, for instance, but who did a better job than any craftsmen in Helsinki would have done. The design was accepted as I had designed it for myself. I'm happy with the way it reacts to the weather and the light. Earlier, when I was a young architect, I thought of architecture as an aesthetic object, but for the last twenty-five years I have thought of it as a condition or way to amplify the nature of things. I'm more concerned with what the building does to one's way of receiving a place.

"At the House of Silence, the geometry of the two curves—one pushing outwards from the slope, the other digging into the slope—was to give two experiences in relation to the landscape, one moving outwards, the other "hiding." The horizontal windows are all for the purpose of pulling you further into the forest, and the rhythm of the trees is around you. In the living room I think it worked quite powerfully. In the sauna, the idea was to place the horizon directly at eye level, and then placing your vision so that it escapes through the narrow channel. I am interested in the mental and psychological impact of the close view, the middle view, and the distant view, and the possibility of shifting between them. The idea of the fireplace is to give a close view, then move to the distant. I think such experiences are deeply rooted and related to the sources of ultimate pleasure."

A terrace extends along three sides of the main house at Ritva Puotila's summer home in the Saimaa lake area, with a sauna contained beneath and giving out onto the water's edge (facing page). Trees have been encouraged to grow as close to the house as possible to make it blend in with the natural forested scenery. The "summer kitchen" of the house (left and far left) has one open corner, while the work surfaces are constructed from wooden slats from a derelict barn. A hurricane lamp stands ready; there is no electric lighting.

KARELIAN SPIRITS ARE KEPT ALIVE AT A SAIMAA SUMMER HOME

A traditional Karelian preference for company and sociability is at the heart of the summer home belonging to textile artist Ritva Puotila and her family in the Saimaa lake region. Ritva Puotila was born in the city of Viipuri before Finland's conflicts with the Soviet Union that ended in 1944. As part of Finland's settlement with its eastern neighbor, it was required to cede Viipuri and much of the surrounding area of Karelia to the Soviets. Ritva is one of the many Finns whose families moved west to reside within Finland's redrawn boundaries.

The Puotila home, occupying one side of a two hectare island and accessible only by boat from the shoreline just over half a mile away, is in fact comprised of a scattering of small buildings, allowing a private family community to thrive here throughout the enchanted, light-flooded summers among the tree-covered slopes and rocky shorelines. The house is quite concealed by trees and invisible to boaters on the lake. The town of Savonlinna can be reached across the same stretch of water.

From the principal jetty, the visitor approaches the main house from the western side, passing a small building with a turf roof containing beds for guests. Behind the main house stands a two hundred-year-old outhouse from southern Karelia, also containing sleeping quarters—a structure that was dissembled from its original site and reconstructed here. This was done in the manner of many traditional outdoor museums of old buildings in the Nordic area, such as the Seurasaari Open Air Museum in Helsinki. These guest quarters are a short distance from the main house, approached from the northern and eastern sides along a terrace that also extends to the southern side overlooking the lake.

Birch, pine, and alder trees screen the sides of the house, increasing its sense of mystery. The trees have been encouraged to grow through the planks of the terrace structure, very close to the house, so the landscape continues to evolve from year to year, changing the character of the house.

A second, lower level is concealed below the southern side of the house, and the home's main sauna is contained here, nestling against the natural slope that leads down to the lakeside beach. The fireplace for the sauna stove, located at its rear, extends up through the center of the main room and through a chimney to the roof.

"We have no electricity at the summer home, and my grandchildren—I have seven—have begged us never to bring electricity here," says Ritva Puotila. The family uses candles and oil lamps for lighting, adding to the intimacy of the atmosphere, and gas for cooking in the compact kitchen area. The design of the main room in the main house further enhances

A HOUSE ON THE LAKE

Proximity to the lake's edge is an integral aspect of the eastern Finnish summer home, and the Saimaa system is the biggest in the whole country, as well as one of the largest in Europe. Wooden pathways (facing page) lead down to a jetty where a vigorously-scrubbed rug hangs drying in the sunshine. Below, a younger member of the family descends the wooden steps for a cooling dip. Unlimited space, water, and forest: the simple natural elements make an impression on the Finnish child, whose appreciation of the beauty of nature will persist into adulthood.

this intimacy. A long communal table extends along one side of the fireplace, while bunk beds and a cooking space line two of the other walls, with the entrance, from the east, on the fourth. The original family of Ritva, her husband, and her children would sleep together in the same room, in the true spirit of a close-knit family community.

A flight of wooden steps leads down from the western side of the house to the water's edge, and the lake laps close to the sauna porch. Also to the west of the main house is a grassy area for children's games and a children's house, with a tower-top room approached by means of more wooden steps. Beyond this is what Ritva calls her "summer kitchen"— a 320-square-foot (30-m²) structure with glass walls forming one corner, a day bed, a magnificent tree-root table, and an open corner, designed as such by Ritva herself to give tangibility to the natural elements. This kitchen—actually conceived as a separate dining room rather than strictly a place to prepare meals—is situated in a small cleft or "canyon," and the views from its various sides are of rock, of sand leading to the lakeside, and of forest.

The gray, weathered tones of the *kelohonka*—the dead standing pine trunks that provide especially sturdy material for log cabins and chalets in Finland—and the rough and earthy textures are also reminiscent of the Woodnotes paper yarn furniture and fittings pioneered by Ritva Puotila, whereby she explicitly expresses the exposed and idiosyncratic character and colors of the essential Finnish landscape.

Completing the complex is a second turf-roofed sauna—the smoke sauna variety, where the occupant is immersed in sooty smoke from the stove. The soot is then used to scour the skin, a process that raises non-Finnish eyebrows but whose efficacy is unquestioned in Finnish sauna lore. Naturally, the smoke sauna is also close to the lake, into which bathers can take an immediate dip.

TRADITION AND MODERNITY:
HOLIDAY HOUSES ON THE ISLANDS

Finland contains the largest archipelago in Europe, with tens of thousands of large and small islands scattered along the coast. The archipelago offers a variety of landscapes, from an undulating softness to a wild coastline cut out of granite where time has polished the rocks silky smooth.

The Finns are deeply attached to the calm landscape of the lakes, but also to the sheltered coast of small islands that, during most of the year, can only be accessed by boat or by a series of small ferries. It is often said that the Finns define themselves as either "island people" or "lake people."

While the modest economic activities of these islands may have declined, a new community–equally vigorous in its own way–has taken over. The archipelago remains one of the most ruggedly beautiful, tranquil, and sparsely-populated regions in Europe, resulting in an influx of city-dwellers in the summer months. From the first warm days of the year, they rush to their *mökki*—or country houses—to witness the blossoming of nature. Far from everything, weekends and holidays are inevitably spent on these islands. In the past, families left the cities on the first of June, only to return home for the beginning of the school year. However, the trend now is to make more frequent trips of shorter duration, allowing visitors to discover the charm of the archipelago in all seasons. The autumn storms are violent but spectacular, with the winds sweeping the golden and rust-colored leaves. Winter is also a popular time to visit the islands. Many newly-constructed summer residences and renovated fishing cabins are now winterized. However, the thick layer of ice near the coast often makes access difficult, forcing visitors to follow the "snow routes" marked out on the frozen sea, or to borrow a snowmobile or hydrocopter.

On the islands, beautiful modern houses blend with the natural surroundings and with the charming, traditional houses also built from wood. Next to little red houses—cottages, saunas, grandmothers' *mökki*—stand the more stately yellow homes. At one time, everything was painted with a natural, soil-based paint that was extremely resistant. In the archipelago, the houses are constructed from boards, and not from *kelohonka* logs that are commonly used along the lakes and in Lapland. Battered by the sea and the salt air, the wooden boards are more resistant to the elements and the humidity than the logs. In the Inkoo archipelago—just 37 miles (60 km) from the capital—the tradition of old-style houses remains strong. The village boasts a beautiful open-air museum that delineates the various types of historical construction. Previously, approximately sixty people lived on this ancient property that unites fishing and fish cultivation. However, the fishermen and farmers have now returned to the mainland,

HOLIDAYS ON THE ISLANDS

*This archipelago landscape of rocky islands is typical of the
fragmented southern Baltic coast of Finland (right).
Holiday homes are scattered throughout the archipelago, where
Finnish families enjoy an easy-going privacy, soaking up every
possible moment of the precious summer sun (below).*

HOLIDAYS ON THE ISLANDS
The largest houses in the archipelago are often painted yellow (above), a feature that—according to tradition—distinguishes the important and imposing houses from the more modest structures.
Facing page: The villa offers spectacular views of the Gulf of Finland (bottom right), which can also be admired from inside the sauna while you soak your feet in the water (bottom left). The furniture of all of these houses is practical and comfortable (top), encouraging the simple joys of reading, a game of cards, or a conversation between friends.

and the property has been transformed into a holiday home with a number of smaller guest houses.

The Finnish summer follows the rhythm of what nature has to offer. The Finns spend their time fishing pike or perch, indulging in the delights of the sauna, never tiring of the splendid sunsets viewed from their terraces. After beginning the day with a revitalizing dip in the sea, it is most relaxing to stretch out on the sun-baked rocks. Popular summertime pastimes include reading, picking bilberries, and gathering mushrooms in the woods. The summer is also the perfect time to teach children how to fish, sail, and live in harmony with the elements. In the archipelago, children are taught to navigate and to read maritime charts from a very young age. The end of summer is the occasion to get together for the most important event of the Finnish gastronomical year: the crayfish festival. An invitation to taste these shellfish is one of the finest compliments a Finn can bestow upon another. These shellfish come exclusively from Finnish rivers and lakes and are, as a result, particularly prized. The celebratory tables are prepared with great care—decorated with candles and a red and white motif to complement the crayfish that are served cold after being cooked in a salted, dill-based broth. This ritual is toasted with glasses of Koskenkorva, a Finnish vodka made from potatoes.

In this technologically-advanced nation, most of the country houses have neither running water nor any other modern comforts. Water is collected from the well, wood is cut to heat the sauna, candles and oil lamps provide the only source of light, and fish is smoked over woodchips in a small smoking room.

The entire coast is strewn with charming villages—such as Nauvo in the Turku archipelago and Rosala in the Hittis—that serve the needs of the island inhabitants. Each has its own summer exhibitions, concerts, and small market, where news is exchanged and shoppers seek out the sweet-tasting black bread that is the ideal accompaniment to smoked halibut.

VILLA UUNILA:
AN AESTHETIC CHALLENGE
TO BUILDING CONVENTIONS

A peculiar house for an extremely unusual person: that is how architect Panu Kaila describes the Villa Uunila which he designed for his friend, Arto Uunila, at Kokemäki, close to Pori in western Finland. With its false perspectives and pleasing natural details, the villa is fondly described by its creator as "a house that is full of ideas."

"I first made some sketches for Arto in the 1980s," recalls Panu. These sketches were for a farm near Ilmajoki in central Finland where Arto had a traditional paint factory. Then he moved his factory to Kokemäki, bought a five-hectare farm site and called Panu again to ask him to design a house. The house, with some renovations made to accommodate the children who live there, remains inhabited by the family of Arto's son, who is now also the owner of the paint business.

"I have known Arto for a long time and I know that no ordinary kind of house would be good enough for him and that he would want something special," says Panu. "I also knew he would be keen to pay attention to the details of the design. Even so, he said I could sketch it quite freely, but that it was to be a representational house for the paint factory."

Panu remembers that, in its early years, the house was used a venue for concerts, theater, and municipal receptions. "It was half home, half meeting place," he says. "Tourist bus excursions heading for other destinations would stop off here and people would visit the house. But importantly, at the same time it represented the paints made at Arto's factory. There is a red part, a yellow part, and a green part, painted like that to demonstrate how your own house might look if painted in those colors."

VILLA UUNILA
The top floor of Villa Uunila's four-sided tower (left) affords views on every side, with small balconies on two sides. The façades of the tower—two of which are of pine and two of spruce—are quite untreated by paint or varnish of any kind. Arto Uunila—the owner of a successful paint factory— deliberately intended to demonstrate that paint is in fact mere decoration for the most part. The wood matures and ages gradually into a natural gray.

VILLA UUNILA

*A small façade of Villa Uunila is constructed
of birch trunks, complete with shimmering white bark (right).
All conventional Finnish building wisdom eschews the use of
birch as a building material, but Arto Uunila and Panu Kaila
have demonstrated that simple, natural elements (facing page)
can be aesthetically pleasing, surprisingly durable, and easily
replaced. The villa also makes creative use of recycled housing
elements, including window frames (far right).
The tall glass wall forming one side of the villa's main room
draws in light and overlooks orchards and meadows leading
down to a river (page 102), while wooden benches and pillars
underline the rustic ambiance (page 103).*

Panu relished the opportunity offered by the site on a small hill at the top of a sloping meadow. Most of the old farm buildings, including the cowshed and stables, had been demolished, and Panu's creation made ingenious use of the remnants of the farmstead. Through the tall glass wall forming one side of the villa's main hall, a view extends to trees in the garden, across the meadow to the road and, finally, to a river.

"When the house was planned, Arto thought of buying an old house in disrepair to demolish and use the materials," says Panu. In the event the actual site provided plenty of material for recycling and this is incorporated, for example, in the windows of the dominant tower. Material from further afield is also used, such as shingle tiles from an old church.

Although the tower is a common feature of Nordic rural villa architecture, the tower of Villa Uunila was conceived with a particularly therapeutic aesthetic in mind. Panu refers to the psychology of a building, completed by the layers from the cellar to the tower's top floor. "At the top of the tower you are above the troubles of everyday life, and it clearly works. You are able to see that all your troubles are not so big, that you can manage and handle things. It gives you a sense of freedom."

The wood of the tower is completely untreated. "Arto's colleagues in the paint trade warned him that the wood would start to deteriorate immediately, but Arto told them this was nonsense, that strong wood does not need to be painted," remembers Panu. He backed up this argument by including inside the house a gray log wall that had been exposed to the elements for one hundred years and had suffered only a few cracks. Creative use of wood is also demonstrated in the pine and birch pillars of the interior—the masculine and feminine elements, as Panu describes them—with the bark in place.

"I learned this technique in Japan, where I worked as a researcher," says Panu. "The tendency today is that everything has to be as durable as possible, but one of the ideas at Villa Uunila is that it is more important to be able to reconstruct the elements easily." At the same time, many of the elements are more durable than may be initially supposed.

VILLA SAGA
A fireplace, fashioned from stone collected from the site, provides
an affable focus for the main room of the Villa Saga. The
window looks out on a wooden terrace—bathed in light in
summer and heaped with snow in winter—from which the sea
may be glimpsed glimmering behind the pine and spruce trees.

VILLA SAGA REVEALS A PERSONAL
TOUCH BY ARCHITECT PEKKA HELIN

As one of Finland's most famous architects abroad and the winner of numerous architectural competitions, Pekka Helin is especially renowned for his large-scale conspicuous works, including Nokia House (Nokia's head office in Espoo) and the extension to the Finnish Parliament in Helsinki. In partnership until 1999 with Tuomo Siitonen, Helin has notched up no fewer than twenty-seven first prizes in competitions, the staging of which has been a cornerstone of Finland's modern approach to architecture.

It is therefore enlightening to take a look at his more intimate and private oeuvre. Helin is no stranger to residential architecture, and new quarters of Helsinki—such as the Laivapoika apartments in Ruoholahti—are rightly celebrated for their freshness and optimism. But individual assignments like the Villa Saga on the island of Ersholmen in southern Finland bear a more personal signature.

The island is part of the Hiitinen coastal archipelago and its south-facing and seaward aspect is in accordance with the residents' request to be confronted with the untempered natural environment. The deliberate absence of any clear shelter means that the house is exposed to all the contrasting whims of the changing seasons, from the invigorating glare of high summer sun to the moody monotones of winter and the relentless gales of spring and fall.

VILLA SAGA

The Villa Saga (below) is assembled from, and stands in harmony with, the same natural components of wood and stone that compose the rugged archipelago landscape of southern Finland. The terracing leading down from the house prevents wear to the rocks, and provides a series of level surfaces for leisure activities. Down at the water's edge (right), where driftwood is chopped on the granite shoreline, the rock remains exposed to the extreme elements of the Finnish annual cycle.

VILLA SAGA

*The kitchen of Villa Saga (above) uses maple—an unusual
choice in a country where pine is a common material.
Facing page, top: The view from the
upper balcony terrace faces south towards the
Bengtskär lighthouse, and the sweep of southern light
seems to infiltrate all corners of the house.
Facing page, bottom: The furniture is most often made of
wood, as a reminder of the proximity to the forest.*

Helin's description is of "an artifact planted and rooted with a gentle hand into the delicate organism, as if becoming part of it," and the design demonstrates a respect for the environmental setting as well as a readiness to realize its full potential. Sympathy with nature is ensured by the use of wood for the main frame, and walls constructed from stones collected from the site itself. The gray board of the façades, coated with non-toxic natural wax, is a reference to the tones of rock and lichen, while the green copper roof blends with the pine, spruce, and other foliage surrounding the site. The house is arranged in three basic units, the two to the east aligned with each other and the one to the west at a slight angle, helping to create a sense of privacy in the terraced aprons extending to the south, above the sea. These enclosed aprons are boarded over to prevent wear to the underlying rock face. A separate sauna building—in addition to the sauna in the villa itself—is discreetly placed some distance to the west along the island's rocky shoreline, while a path leads down to a private jetty to the east.

The interior of the house finds Helin lending a sensitive ear to the tastes and requirements of the villa's residents. Wood is the dominant material, with broad planks of Douglas fir composing much of the floor and maple used for the kitchen fixtures. Quartzite slabs form the floor in the entrance and there is a rough stone fireplace. The differing heights of the rooms result from the differing levels, which follow the natural lie of the land.

Upstairs, the sauna and bedroom extend onto a balcony above the broad terrace, and on a clear day the maritime panorama reaches to the Bengtskär lighthouse. Passing yachtsmen looking back at the house from the sea may catch a glimpse of reflected sunlight from the window, but the house blends so effectively into the landscape as to be almost indistinguishable from it.

HISTORY BROUGHT TO LIFE
IN THE TARNA HOME IN PORVOO

A corner parlor at the house of Liisa and Tauno Tarna in the Old Town
of Porvoo has a colorful distinction: this was where Czar Alexander I of
Russia took tea on a visit during the 1809 Diet of Porvoo, at which
Finland's autonomous status within the Russian Empire was enshrined,
paving the way for the independence achieved in 1917.

For the Tarna couple, this footnote to Finnish history is part of the
period character they have taken great pains to preserve in what is now
their home. The wooden house stands on one side of the square opposite
the dominating church (which was granted cathedral status in the
eighteenth century) and near the top of a slope scattered with historic
wooden houses leading down to the river. The house was built in 1792
for a merchant by the name of Solitander, whose ships imported goods
from Tallinn and Lübeck in the Baltic and as far away as Liverpool. One
section of the house on the square served as a shop at which these goods
were offered for sale; the shop was open only on Sunday mornings to
attract worshippers departing from services at the church.

The plan of the two-floor house is typical of the Swedish influence
prevalent at the time of construction, with smaller rooms radiating from
a large central drawing room in a rough "L" shape. The vertical wood
cladding that covers the exterior is also typical of the Swedish style.
There are hints of Russian influence too, not least in the green pigment
of the paint that dominates outside and which has also been detected in
the original paints used for the exteriors.

"Solitander had many connections with Saint Petersburg, where green was a favorite color for houses," explains Tauno. "When Solitander painted his house green, all the other houses in the town were painted red!" The appearance of the house was thus a statement of its owner's affluence and influence.

Liisa and Tauno, by profession an interior architect with a special interest in the restoration of old properties, spent ten years renovating it and filling it with period furniture and fittings. The structure is based on a vaulted cellar that predates the present house by more than a century—the only remains of a building destroyed by one of a succession of fires that razed earlier incarnations of the Old Town. The walls in the cellar are of Dutch brick, imported as ballast by ships from Holland that came to Porvoo to collect loads of timber and tar.

"The costs of conservation work were high," Tauno recalls. "But I bought nothing new from the shops in the trade. Instead, I used discarded materials, such as handmade nails and timber, from other renovations or demolitions. Modern facilities, in the kitchen, for example, were installed, but hidden so that they do not disturb the original plan."

The rooms of the house, which include three low-ceilinged bedrooms on the second floor, contain eleven original Swedish tiled stoves, all of which are in working order. Thirteen layers of decorative paper were revealed on one wall of the drawing room during the preservation project; other walls were covered with new canvas, in accordance with the eighteenth-century procedure, and new paint applied.

Russian Empire and Gustavian, or Louis XVI, furniture sits beside modern ornaments and sculptures, providing a surprisingly successful contrast, as well as a reminder that the Tarnas have achieved an attractive and comfortable hybrid of a museum and a living, breathing home.

MERCHANT'S HOUSE, PORVOO
Antiques contrast brilliantly with contemporary Finnish art in the Solitander house. A ceramic work by Johanna Rytkölä and an Oiva Toikka glass ornament are placed near a traditional Swedish tiled stove (above).
Facing page: Oiva Toikka eggs, and a granite torso by Marjo Lahtinen (top) grace the drawing room with black and white paintings by Päivi Sirén. A set of Russian Empire furniture decorated with swans (bottom left), a a Louis XVI chair (bottom center), and Gustavian furniture (bottom right), emphasize the period atmosphere in other rooms.

NATURAL SPONTANEITY AT VILLA LÅNGBO

An irreverent twinkle illuminates the eyes of architect Olavi Koponen as he describes Villa Långbo, the dwelling that he designed and built on an island in Finland's southwestern archipelago. The spontaneity evident in the building is a quality that its creator appears to relish.

Built in phases between 1994 and 1999, Villa Långbo is some thirty-seven miles (60 km) from the city of Turku on the western tip of an island that measures just over a mile (2 km) in length and a third of a mile (0.5 km) in width. The villa was intended as a place to live at any time of the year—not only as a holiday home—and it bears little immediate resemblance to the traditional Finnish concept of the shoreside leisure cottage. Located at the top of a high and relatively exposed rocky outcrop overlooking the sea, about sixty-six feet (20 m) above sea level, familiar elements are hard to discern.

On the edge of the forest and partly obscured by it, a set of pine "boxes" are aligned beneath a corrugated roof with an apparent fragility that is deceptive. As the wind rises, the viewer could be forgiven for fearing that the villa might collapse and swirl like tumbleweed. The pine shingles that cover the sauna element glow like fall leaves in the afternoon summer sun, and look as if they would flutter to the ground as easily. This illusion is part of the genius of Villa Långbo and is in line with the idea of dissolving the boundaries between the building and its natural context.

In fact, the villa is anchored on a firm and steady platform. "When I first came here, there was nothing but nature," recalls Koponen. "Usually when I start to design something, I have to get a philosophical idea of it, of what the building is doing in that place. I thought that when humans arrive in that kind of place, they usually occupy part of that natural environment. That's why I decided to make a big platform and to place the elements of the villa on the platform, then put the shared roof over that. If people are living on such a platform, they don't destroy the nature around the platform."

The original plans for the building were for a single, 130-foot- (40 m-) long element, but this evolved—through both the organic process of

VILLA LÅNGBO
Pine shingles are an unusual covering for the sauna at Villa Långbo, yet the structure is less fragile than it would seem. The sauna is one of several box-like units sandwiched between a continuous roof and an elevated platform.

VILLA LÅNGBO

Villa Långbo provides elements of privacy and sociability by combining intimate and segregated areas with comfortable shared space (facing page). The slate fireplace (right), for example, is a natural focus for assembling, while the hammock outside the sauna (far right) provides a quiet spot for contemplating the view of the sea.

adapting to the actual location and the requirements of planning permission—into a three-sided configuration. The western "wing" looks out across the sea and its elevation allows it to bask in the full beam of the setting sun. The sauna and mainly glass-walled lounge, as well as a fireplace constructed from stacked black slate, are located here. Three bedrooms are arranged to the north, and two more rooms and a library comprise the eastern side of the yard, which encloses a jacuzzi. Koponen has aimed to imbue each room with its own distinct identity, defined by its relation to natural light and its setting.

"I thought of the villa as a place not only for holidays," he explains. "People need to be together but they also need to be alone, and you need both elements in life at any time. This box configuration allows you to have your own world, and there are common, shared areas too. Secondly, there is the connection between people and nature. When I saw pictures of this villa later in magazines and books, I felt that the house looks very strange, even to myself. You cannot see where the house starts exactly. It doesn't have a clear shape; it's very much like part of the construction of nature. It is even stranger than I imagined it would be.

"I understand that some people will say this is not architecture in the usual sense. When it was covered in a Finnish architectural magazine, the editor said that a lot of architects called him and asked: 'How is it possible for this magazine to cover this kind of building?'" Koponen relates the story with a gentle laugh, enjoying the reaction that the villa can inspire.

Koponen's concern for natural harmony, of course, is far from rebellious and quite in tune with instinctive Finnish traditions and the more conscious, modern regard for the natural environment. He makes one playful reference to his own rural childhood in the Savo region of Finland in the placing of a dark chamber in the northeastern corner of the villa. Small slit windows provide the only illumination for this unit, a refuge for calm and private contemplation. He explains the design as follows: "When I was a child I lived in the countryside and I remember when my parents were working in the fields that we slept in the barn and shafts of light came in through the logs."

The villa is insulated normally, heated electrically, and provided with a water supply. It could therefore be occupied at any time of the year. The relatively mild Finnish winters in recent years, however, have made access in this season problematic: the sea ice is often too fragile to support the weight of a human, but too thick to allow the passage of a small boat. During the winters of its construction, however, the ice was sufficiently thick to allow a team of horses to assist in transporting materials from the mainland—an image that Koponen fondly recalls.

"Spontaneity is important here," he concludes. "If you aim for a relaxed feeling, you ought to plan it in a relaxed manner. There ought to be some uncertainty. If everything is in the right place and according to plan, the chances are that it will not be relaxed."

A HINT OF BAROQUE AT LEMSJÖHOLM

The Lemsjöholm manor, situated on a peninsula about twenty-five miles (40 km) northwest of the city of Turku, was built in 1767 by Herman Fleming. Fleming was also the owner of the Louhisaari manor, known in Swedish as Villnäs, built in 1653–1655. Louhisaari—an unusually palatial manor for the region—later became the home of the Mannerheim family and the birthplace of the marshal of Finland, Carl Gustav Mannerheim.

The histories of the manors are closely related and they are situated near to each other. Fleming bought Lemsjöholm in 1764 and it is believed that Christian Friedrich Schröder, the city architect of Turku at that time, was the designer of the manor.

The plastered house, built primarily of brick, has a very high mansard roof and gabled windows on three floors. Because of its high, narrow proportions, it conveys a dignified, almost baroque impression, and is a far cry from the mixture of rococo and French classicism that characterize Schröder's other famous buildings. The plan design, accounting for eighteen rooms, also resembles the layout of Louhisaari, suggesting that Fleming had set his heart on a similar house.

In 1823 Lemsjöholm was acquired by Lars Gabriel von Haartman, one of the most important representatives of Finland during the reign of Russian Czar Nicholas I, being governor of Finland as a Grand Duchy, senator, and prime minister. Von Haartman in turn married two of the Mannerheim sisters from Louhisaari and he is the great-great grandfather of the present owner, Jan von Haartman.

Much of the interior remains intact from the days of the original von Haartman inhabitants. The house was a popular venue for parties and social gatherings of the occupants of neighboring manors, as well as other friends and family through the nineteenth century. There also evolved a hunting tradition that endures today. Lemsjöholm remains the private family home of what is now the fifth generation of von Haartmans, and has been carefully restored in recognition of its historical importance as an example of architecture from the period when Finland still lay under Swedish administration.

LEMSJÖHOLM
*The dining room
at Lemsjöholm retains
the atmosphere of its
mid-eighteenth-century
origins. A handsome
rococo tiled stove
dominates the corner;
rococo chairs, portraits of
Swedish kings and queens,
items of Qianlong
porcelain, and early
nineteenth-century pewter
candlesticks complete
the period scene.*

HOUSE INTO

Steel struts supporting the House Into extend down to the rock like the roots of a powerful plant (far right). The spiral staircase (facing page) complements the natural grain of the wood. The seaward view is reflected in the tall, glazed walls and in the indoor swimming pool (following double page) where one can enjoy the illusion of diving into the sky.

BALANCE OF DETAIL AT HOUSE INTO IN ESPOO

House Into in Espoo, just to the west of Helsinki, is an expression of the idea of architect Jyrki Tasa that "the materials and details closest to the dweller are an essential element in architecture: what we touch and grasp." Tasa has stated that his main aim for this project was "to find a balance between large, clear elements and small details." These elements and details are made from wood, metal, and glass and retain a sense of naturalness wherever possible, combining the strength and dynamism of steel with the gentler rhythm of wood.

The house faces west and the Baltic sea, shunning the dark north for the warm southern rotation of the sun. It stands isolated on a large exposed platform of rock, and the visitor gains an increased sense of privacy on approach by the steel bridge that leads to a glass entrance in a dazzling white wall. Upon entering, an immediate view presents itself through the facing glass wall, with the sea visible beyond a wide terraced area.

The rest of the house—the bedrooms and sauna to the left, a swimming pool to the right—can be acknowledged as one enters. A first floor kitchen gives way to a dining area and an outdoor balcony, while another sun balcony opens out from the living room to the right. In any season, the tall glazed walls draw in the precious light that brings life to the tones of pine plywood and, in the kitchen, cherry.

The forty-six-foot (14-m) white concrete tower that extends from the center of the house increases the sense of light and houses two soapstone fireplace stoves that open onto the swimming pool on one floor and the living room on the other. The rest of the structure is made from steel frames connected by wooden frames and beams, vertical steel tubes, and wooden roof beams supported by stainless steel columns and beams.

The house, with its concise bedrooms and utility space, was conceived as the ultimate bachelor pad, but it is sufficiently expansive in its shared space to encourage social gatherings. Standing on the balcony, drink in hand, the summer sun glinting on an apron of sea, the guest at the House Into could be forgiven for thinking that Helsinki's rumbling metropolis were a thousand miles away, not just twelve (20 km).

RENDEZVOUS IN FINLAND

Finnish architect Jukka Sirén describes one extreme of Finnish archtecture as being marked by "modesty and simplicity combined with craftsmanship," and an attention to detail that seeks a harmony between the different elements of a building and its setting.

Modesty, simplicity, and harmony are elements in evidence across the whole Finnish spectrum—not just, as Sirén says, at one extreme— of building, design and, by extension, leisure-time comforts. The Finnish lifestyle embraces luxury of an uncomplicated nature, and this approach finds expression in the honest hospitality of its hotels, for instance. Finland's restaurants, whose range, variety, and imagination increase with each passing year, welcome international ideas in their design and menus, yet the most successful and attractive pay recognizable homage to traditional principles.

The crafts of the architect and the designer are respected here, and their arts are interwoven in the fabric of the country's heritage. That heritage includes stout stone and wooden churches as well as sleek modern chapels and reconstructed museum villages of traditional and humble wooden buildings alongside granite edifices that house ancient artifacts. Manor houses are scattered through the wooded countryside, while Finland's imposing castles loom above sea and lake—perfect settings for myths and romance.

EHRENSVÄRD MUSEUM AND LOUHISAARI MANOR
The Ehrensvärd Museum (page 128) on Helsinki's island fortress of Suomenlinna is housed in the former Commander's quarters and its Gustavian furniture and portraits tell the story of Finland's period of Swedish rule. The Louhisaari Manor (left, far left, and right) is a magnificent—if unusual—example of central European-style and seventeenth-century palatial architecture in Finland.

MUSEUMS

Tradition and contemporary architecture are the very essence of life in Finland and are central to the many and varied museums that are open to visitors.

Louhisaari Manor, in the municipality of Askainen (Villnäs in Swedish) in southwestern Finland, is the kind of architectural and historical surprise that makes an exploration of the country's less frequented and sparsely populated rural regions so worthwhile. Its three-storied, dignified, whitewashed façade towers above the surrounding English-style landscaped parkland, its palatial grace conveying more than a hint of central European traditions. The grand style of the central manor building and the late Renaissance symmetry completed by its annexes and courtyard are very rare in Finnish architecture.

The main building dates from 1655, but parts of the annex buildings, such as the basement of the southeastern outhouse, are believed to have sixteenth-century origins. The estate was mentioned in records in the fifteenth century, at the end of which it belonged to the noble Kurki family. It is known that the opposite annex housed the bakery and kitchen facilities until 1792. The entire complex was renovated and repaired in the eighteenth century; after further restorations in the 1960s, the exteriors once again present their original seventeenth-century faces to the world.

Visitors are attracted by the fact that Louhisaari was the birthplace in 1867 and subsequent childhood home of one of the pillars of Finnish history, Carl Gustaf Mannerheim, wartime leader and chosen by Parliament as one of the earliest leaders of independent Finland in 1919. The Mannerheim family had acquired Louhisaari from the Flemings, an influential dynasty in the Swedish administration of Finland from the sixteenth to the eighteenth centuries. One Herman Fleming, who died in 1573, conceived other local plans predating the manor, including that for the chapel some two miles (3 km) away at Askainen.

The manor's second floor, which was originally the main residential space, has been restored to its eighteenth- and nineteenth-century glory, while the first and second story interiors reflect the seventeenth-century phase of the manor's evolution. The interiors are graced with furniture whose shades and upholstery have been restored, but none of the original fittings installed by the Fleming family remain on show.

Many of the manors of southern Finland are the legacy of the country's earliest industrialists, whose exploitation of the potential of the area's fast-flowing rivers dates back to the seventeenth century. Many well-preserved relics remain in the form of mill and village complexes constructed around rapids and near the forest resources felled for charcoal to heat the early furnaces. As an integral part of the Swedish Empire until the early nineteenth century, Finland had access

to resources across that empire; pig iron and ore were imported from Sweden to the foundries of Strömfors, Fagervik, Mustio, Billnäs, and Fiskars, to name the best-known.

Strolling through the valley at Fiskars, where a string of wooden workers' dwellings and industrial buildings runs along the river, the visitor may well wonder whether, a century on, the industrial milieus of the twenty-first century will be as quaint as this. Indeed, the contemporary sense of picturesque calm belies the erstwhile hardships endured by the original seventeenth-century workforce, whose humble wooden houses have acquired a retrospective appeal.

The village dates to 1649 when Dutch industrialists built the first blast furnace there, setting the foundations of an industry that was to endure well into the twentieth century, when the Fiskars name became globally synonymous with ergonomically designed orange-handled scissors and garden tools. The roots of the Fiskars company are firmly planted here and it is a heritage proudly celebrated in the museums and handicraft shops that occupy many of the buildings. A community of craftspeople, artists, and designers has taken up the creative mantle, ensuring that Fiskars the village—like Fiskars the brand—will continue to be associated with progressive innovation. Many of the buildings have been renovated and reoccupied, and what could have become a sterile but attractive backwater enjoys a new life as a thriving and repopulated, fully functioning village.

Most of the village as it is preserved today was built to the designs of the nineteenth-century foundry owner, John von Julin, whose reputation as an enlightened employer is equaled by his apparent regard for empathy with the natural environment. In von Julin's day, of course, a pall of smoke would have hung over the main foundries, and the calm would have been broken by the clank and hiss of the now-closed railway running to the harbor at Pohjankuru. But the succession of glassy pools and frothing rapids, and the grassy banks and dipping trees, are preserved as integral aspects of the milieu's entity.

Other traditional milieus can be visited at the Open Air Museum of Seurasaari in Helsinki. Seurasaari occupies a thickly wooded island to the northwest of Helsinki city center. It is linked to the mainland by a long white wooden bridge, the approach to which is close to the former home (now a museum) of the late President Urho Kekkonen, a scattering of quaint wooden villas, and a branch of the Helsinki City

LOUHISAARI MANOR
The whitewashed palatial Louhisaari Manor (above) is an architectural surprise in the Finnish landscape, and a very rare example of its style in this part of the world. Facing page: The furniture and fittings in the middle floor (top) are representative of the eighteenth and nineteenth centuries, while the top floor (bottom) has retained its seventeenth-century character.

FISKARS

Exhibition space in the old foundry village of Fiskars, itself the home of many artists and designers, provides an inspirational setting for artists from Finland and further afield in which to present their work. The White exhibition at the Granary (facing page), for example, included works by Sakari Kannosto and Riitta Talonpoika, while a ceramics show at the Copper Smithy (below) featured works by the likes of Daniel Pontoreau and Pekka Paikkari.

SEURASAARI

The simple rustic artistry of the traditional furniture at the Seurasaari Open Air Museum in Helsinki (facing page) is an early example of efficient practicality in Finnish design. The Florin summer house (right) hints at a more elaborate neoclassical influence.

Museum of Art. As you step onto the bridge, the dim roar of the city recedes and you are gradually drawn into a rural haven, where tame red squirrels scamper up to the feet of children and glimpses of the silver sea flash through the trees.

On the far shore is an enclosed naturist bathing area, but the rocks and reedy coastline are also popular with more modest bathers. A restaurant stands above a quay where tourist cruise boats call on their summer excursions, and a clearing in the woods stages traditional dancing on Midsummer Eve. Throughout the summer months, guides dressed in traditional costumes offer information and demonstrate time-honored crafts. The buildings lock their doors in the winter, but skiers arrive across the frozen sea and the alluring aroma of grilled sausage wafts through the frosty air.

Entire farmsteads and manors have been rebuilt here, but the buildings are scattered over the gentle slopes of the island, so the visitor stumbles across a barn here, a cottage there. A relaxed and picturesque park for some, Seurasaari is a catalog of Finnish architectural skill and development for others, demonstrating how the demands of climate and country hardships have driven the evolution of practical and durable, yet also hugely appealing design styles.

One of the most charming exhibits is the Karuna Church, which dates from 1685, with a bell tower added in 1767. Oil paintings adorn the walls, the lower parts of which are also painted with patterns, and the Apostles and Christ appear depicted in the organ gallery. The small church is popular with summer weddings, especially at Midsummer, when the chosen newly-weds are taken down to more celebrations by the blazing bonfires on the shore.

The care with which the old buildings have been reconstructed at Seurasaari is one manifestation of public awareness of architecture. The same awareness accounts for the multiple controversies aroused by Helsinki's Museum of Contemporary Art when it was unveiled in 1998. The first debate surrounded the nationality of its architect, Steven Holl, who hails from the USA and whose design was chosen from more than five hundred competition entries. Many lamented the fact that no young Finnish talent was selected for such a prestigious project. The opposing camp recognized the healthy lack of parochialism in opting for an approach that essentially transcended the borders of national traditions, or at any rate, pays little obvious heed to Finnish motifs.

In time, opposition to the museum's design faded, and it has set about its stated business to good effect as a kind of "living room for the city" where citizens can drop in for bites of cultural nourishment. A thriving café and restaurant, with most of the fittings and furniture also designed by Holl, and a compact but excellent art bookshop supplement the cultural diet, and newspapers are strewn on tables for all to read.

Outside, on the apron next to the Mannerheim statue and on the sloping lawn, youngsters bask in the summer sun that bounces back from the museum's shining surface and a stage is erected for outdoor performances.

Holl called his creation Kiasma, which means the crossing point of two lines, implying an interaction between ideas that head in different directions, as well as reflecting the physical shape of the building. Kiasma is now a fixture on the Helsinki landscape, regarded with increasing affection; many people now accept that the vast shadow of Mannerheim on horseback cast across its western façade adds presence to the statue rather than detracts from its effect.

Natural light falls through the untreated glass and bathes the simple white walls that sweep up from the entrance ramp towards the exhibition spaces above. These exhibition spaces are irregular, with swooping arched walls reminiscent of some Greek chapel or monastery, lending a sense of adventure to the visitor's progress through the building. Holl has not lost site of Kiasma's prime purpose—to be a museum of contemporary art—and he has taken account of the low winter light in the angles of his skylights, as well as the saturation of natural illumination that can be captured in the summer months. The broad windows on the north end, with their views across to the trams and cars on the busy road and the Parliament, also give the visitor the sense that the city is being drawn into the museum, not excluded.

A similar welcome is extended in the public libraries of Helsinki and rest of the country. According to different world rankings, Finland sits permanently in the top three countries for 100-percent literacy, and this quality is underlined by the lack of exclusivity in its academic resources of which the National Library of Finland at the Helsinki University Library occupies the apex.

KIASMA MUSEUM OF CONTEMPORARY ART

Visitors to the Kiasma Museum of Contemporary Art in Helsinki are guided to the exhibition areas along a wide ascending ramp (facing page). Architect Steven Holl has amplified ambient light by means of whitewashed walls (below), and the result is a startling, public building whose bold lack of symmetry polarized opinion when it was opened in 1997.

The current collection consists of 2.6 million books and periodicals, in addition to the same number of manuscripts, maps and other documents. The music manuscripts of Jean Sibelius are included here, as are the maps in the library of the explorer A.E. Nordenskiöld and fragments of vellum texts dating back to the twelfth-century.

Originating from the remains of the library at the Royal Academy of Turku, most of which perished in a great fire of 1827, the collection was moved to its Helsinki home in 1828 after the start of Russian rule. Its main building, completed in 1845, remains the handsome Empire-style edifice by C.L. Engel, with its Rotunda annex contributed by Gustaf Nyström in 1906.

But in Helsinki, the relative scarcity of ancient monuments makes the island fortress of Suomenlinna, around a mile off the southern shore, guarding the entrance to the capital's South Harbor, all the more precious. The cobbled paths and ramparts, their cannons now aimed harmlessly at passing cruise ships and Baltic freighters, stretch across a miniature archipelago of half a dozen islands, the southern side of which catches the raw slap of the sea wind, and the northern side of which offers a soothing panorama of the city skyline. Sheltered parks and gardens are protected from the Baltic's wilder elements by the sturdy granite battlements.

These days, the fortress is Helsinki's prime tourist attraction, a magnet for summer picnickers and winter ice-strollers, linked with the main Market Square by a fifteen-minute shuttle ferry crossing. Museums, such as the Ehrensvärd Museum named after the fortress's founder, and restaurants occupy the fortifications, and a small community of permanent inhabitants resides here, along with cadets from a naval academy. Artists hide themselves away in studios, while galleries and shops open in the former arsenals in summer. Traditional wooden ships are repaired in the vast dry dock and vacationing sailors berth their yachts in the marina, stocking up in the island store before continuing to explore the coastline's archipelagos.

Although it was the scene of a precursor of the Russian Revolution in 1906, when the Russian forces staged a mutiny here, the landscape of Suomenlinna today is mostly unchanged since the reconstructions that immediately followed the 1855 bombardment. Its scale, historical importance, beauty, and character are preserved by virtue of its recognition as a UNESCO World Heritage site.

After disembarking from the city ferry, visitors make their way through the pastel-pink main gate on the island of Iso Mustasaari or head for the footbridge to the west that leads across to the naval academy. Beyond the main gate is a little village of wooden villas, their fences a

THE POET'S HOUSE
*The former home of the National Poet, the author of the words
to the Finnish national Anthem, J.L. Runeberg (1804–1877), in
the town of Porvoo reflects the Empire neoclassical style of its
yellow-painted exterior. Runeberg, like his journalist wife
Fredrika, wrote in Swedish, and Sibelius set a number of his
poems to music. The house is one of Finland's earliest museums
and has been open to the public since 1882.*

tangle of Virginia creeper in summer and submerged beneath drifted snow in winter. The paths lead across Iso Mustasaari, passing artillery barracks and other residential areas, then sloping down to the Visitor Center, close to another ferry quay and the bridge to the second main island, Susisaari.

The visitor follows the cobbled path up to another gate, leading off into dungeons to the right, before entering a courtyard containing the grave of Ehrensvärd, surrounded by apartment houses and museum buildings. This is the geographical center and, as the resting place of its founder, the spiritual heart of the fortress.

One route leads down to the dry dock, another continues to the southern and western extremities, including the royal gate with its flight of steps leading down to a small quay. A series of large nineteenth-century Russian cannons crowns the southern battlements, while the shelves of rock below the grassy slopes are favorite sunbathing spots in summer. The ferry trip back to the Market Square provides an exhilarating view of the white Lutheran Cathedral dominating the neoclassical Senate Square.

Helsinki's status as the cultural magnet of Finland is underlined by the annual, late summer Helsinki Festival, the biggest concentration of events and performances on the calendar. Yet the national appetite for culture needs satisfying at venues across the country.

One such venue is the Salmela Art Center, in the village of Mäntyharju close to the banks of Lake Pyhävesi in eastern Finland. The center is distributed through a scattering of renovated wooden buildings dating back to the 1850s, including a former post office and pharmacy. The surrounding parkland is an effective backdrop for sculptures, while shows of art by established and emerging contemporary Finnish artists are presented in the exhibition space. A program

of lectures proceeds through the summer, while concerts by top class performers, ranging right up to the Helsinki Philharmonic Orchestra, are held in the nearby wooden church—the second biggest in Finland—at Mäntyharju.

Finland's cultural traditions are rooted in its history, and friendly provincial rivalries help to maintain their buoyancy. One such rivalry is between the present and previous capitals of the country. The Russian rulers of the newly-appointed nineteenth-century Grand Duchy of Finland wanted a capital that was closer to the center of imperial power in Saint Petersburg to the east, and the previous Finnish capital, Turku, in the south-western corner of the country closest to Sweden, was stripped of the title in favour of Helsinki.

Rather than sulking about its less powerful status, Turku has emerged as a breezy city, an important passenger and cargo port clustered around the mouth of the picturesque banks of the River Aura, with much remaining evidence of a history that predates that of Helsinki. The seven hundred-year-old cathedral is the "Mother Church" of Finnish Lutheranism, for instance, and the thirteenth-century castle, close to the ferry harbor, is splendidly preserved and houses the city's historical museum. On the hillside at Luostarinmäki, a handicrafts museum is distributed over an area of some thirty wooden houses that survived the devastating fire of 1827.

One of Finland's most fascinating museums is close to the River Aura in what was the most select area of the city of Turku in the late seventeenth-century. The Qwensel House is named after its first owner, Wilhelm Johan Qwensel, an associate judge dispatched from Stockholm, the center of empire, to this Finnish outpost. The single storey premises form a long horse-shoe, its flat base facing the riverfront street of Rantakatu, and its eastern and western wings enclosing an extended courtyard. The single entity that exists today is an amalgam of units that evolved over the eighteenth- and nineteenth-centuries, but the Pharmacy Museum that is now housed here dates from 1958. It is a superbly evocative recreation of mainly nineteenth-century apothecary processes, instruments, laboratories, and paraphernalia.

Back to Helsinki, the artistic temperaments of the composer Jean Sibelius and artist Akseli Gallen-Kallela, drew them to the inspirations of the Finnish natural environment. The young architects of the early twentieth century were also keen to find their muse away from the city. The trio of Eliel Saarinen, Armas Lindgren, and Herman Gesellius chose as their retreat a woodland site above a steep slope overlooking the lake of Vitträsk, some sixteen miles (25 km) to the west of central Helsinki. The group of buildings resulting from their endeavors remains as a museum and monument to the folksy and vernacular variation on the Jugendstil known as the Finnish National Romantic.

Hvitträsk (facing page), now a museum and a favorite excursion destination for visitors to Helsinki, was conceived as a studio home in 1901–1903 for the architect team of Eliel Saarinen, Armas Lindgren, and Herman Gesellius, and is an enchanting masterpiece of the Finnish National Romantic strand of art nouveau. The Arts and Crafts movement of the period inspired the residents, who contributed to the design of the furniture, including the bedroom furniture (left) and fittings, as well as the building plans.

Saarinen, Lindgren, and Gesellius were the team responsible for the National Museum in Helsinki, visible from Kiasma's northern windows—a building that is bursting with traditional rural references, including a dominant church-like annex and the granite statue of a bear and other details at its entrance. The three architects conceived Hvitträsk as a combined home and studio away from the city, in touch with the elements of nature on which they drew so richly in their work.

In time, Eliel Saarinen was to outgrow the partnership and by 1907, just six years after the first studio-office was designed, his colleagues had gone their separate ways. In the meantime, Gesellius had married Saarinen's first wife, while Saarinen had married Gesellius's sister. Hvitträsk had become a magnet for Finland's artistic elite, including Sibelius and Gallen-Kallela, and a focus for attempts to define a national identity in the face of Russian domination. Distinguished visitors also came from outside Finland, including Gustav Mahler and Maxim Gorky, and a certain degree of notoriety was achieved for the riotous and competitive drinking sessions that took place here.

Saarinen made some alterations to the buildings and, due to a fire, some rebuilding was also necessary to the house originally occupied by Lindgren. Eliel Saarinen lived at Hvitträsk until 1923, when he traveled to the United States to become one of Finland's—and the world's—most celebrated architects. His grave and that of Gesellius can be found in the woods, close to the group of buildings. Eero, the son of Eliel and Loja Gesellius, became renowned as an architect in his own right.

Hvitträsk is a unique celebration of Finnish interpretations of Art Nouveau and Arts and Crafts styles, where the architects' imaginations ran glorious riot. Three main buildings remain, one of which is used as a restaurant, and a terraced garden spreads to the side of the main house. A long, single-floor studio links the two residential buildings. A lengthy flight of steps, passing through thick forest, leads down to a sauna on the lakeshore.

The house manages to combine the mystery of some mythical Karelian tale, the welcoming security of a home, and the indomitable aspect of a granite castle. The rooflines slope and slant eccentrically, and turrets and balconies lend an air of fantasy. Traditional ryijy rugs, including the striking "Flame" designed by Gallen-Kallela, flamboyant mats, wooden furniture, arched windows, and intricate painted details following the Gothic curve of the ceilings all contribute to a visually aesthetic feast. Copper and iron details in the fireplaces acknowledge the influence of the Belgian designer Henry Van De Velde, while much of the furniture has echoes of Scotland's Charles Rennie Mackintosh.

FINNISH CHURCHES:
THE ROOTS OF AN ARCHITECTURAL HERITAGE

Christianity became established in Finland in the early thirteenth century. Some of the country's churches stand as examples of the earliest Finnish architecture. The English-born St. Henry is credited with bringing the faith to Finland, and many of the first churches were fashioned from stone, thus defying the ravages of fire and decay. It was Mikael Agricola, a bishop of the vast cathedral at Turku, who led Finland—then part of the Swedish Empire—to its conversion to Lutheranism in the sixteenth century, and who also first translated the Bible into Finnish. No medieval pre-Lutheran wooden churches remain, but the landscapes of southern—and particularly southwestern—parts of the country still feature many sturdy stone churches.

The church of Finström in the Åland archipelago, for instance, was built on the site of a wooden church in the thirteenth century, while most of the main church at Porvoo, which has cathedral status, dates to the early fifteenth century. The motifs and designs of stone churches were used as references in the Finnish National Romantic variation on Jugendstil at the end of the nineteenth century and are detectable in buildings like the National Museum and National Theater in Helsinki.

Later wooden churches survive, including the biggest wooden Christian church in the world at Kerimäki in eastern Finland, just over nine miles (15 km) from the lakeland town of Savonlinna. Kerimäki is a small and otherwise insignificant community of some six thousand souls. Incredibly, the village church can seat half of these and standing room is available for a further two thousand. The church's 120-foot- (37-m-) high dome is visible for miles around, and the building dwarfs the settlement that nestles around it.

The church at Kerimäki was designed by the architect A.F. Granstedt and completed in 1847. Popular legend has it that the

PETÄJÄVESI
The circular blue ceiling in the entrance conceals a panel
previously used to lift church bells into place.

PETÄJÄVESI

The pulpit is the most ornate feature of the church in Petäjävesi,
which in many ways is a testament to the simple and pragmatic
character of eighteenth-century Finnish carpentry (below). The
church, consecrated in 1764, was built to replace a smaller chapel
nearby. Facing page: The intricacy of detail in the main church
reveals the remarkable skill of Finnish carpentry, which remains
timeless.

church was erected on such a large scale because of confusion over measurements on the part of the builders. In fact, the enormity was deliberate and based on the request of the local priest, one Fredrik Neovius, who zealously sought to herd together as many of his flock as he could. Though not a big town, Kerimäki held a market and was the gathering place for festivals in the rural neighborhood. With the arrival of the church, it could collect the majority of this congregation for religious worship. The builder, Magnus Tolpo, began the construction, which was completed by his son Theodor, and every able-bodied male in the community between the ages of fifteen and sixty was commandeered to lend a hand in the project.

The resulting, slightly eccentric combination of classical and Gothic is attributed to this collective of relatively unskilled woodworkers, yet the church is a masterpiece of carpentry. If anything, the scale of the church is more striking from the inside, a spaciousness that is emphasized by the light paint shades and the impression of marbling. The pews, measuring a total of nearly 5,600 feet (1,700 m), the cross beams, and other wooden details, including the altar and organ, add to the celebration of woodcraft. The eccentricity, on the other hand, is underlined by the absence of any heating system, rendering such a cavernous space unusable on chilly Finnish winter Sundays. At such times the congregation huddles in the adjacent new church, dating from 1953. Even so, the church is full at Christmas, when the parishioners flood its space with magical candlelight.

The craft of traditional carpentry is showcased at churches throughout Finland. An intimate and unassuming example is to be found at the UNESCO World Heritage-listed Old Church of Petäjävesi in the parish of Jämsä in central Finland. The church is exquisitely located, partially screened by pine and birch trees, and is close to the banks of the small lake from which the village gets its name. The church serves a village of barely four thousand inhabitants and was completed in 1764, according to the plans of master carpenter Jarkko Leppänen, whose son Erkki later built the bell tower in 1821. The cruciform configuration adheres to the Renaissance church plan and details such as the tiny columns decorating the choir screen and galleries repeat this style.

There are Gothic references, however, in the stacked roof, and a shingled exterior forms an attractive pattern on the octagonal dome topping the four-sided, tiered, and shingled bell tower and steeple. Inside, the pulpit is modeled on that of the church's "parent" building in the town of Jämsä, with images of the Evangelists Matthew, Mark, Luke, and John decorating its panels. There is even a whimsical baroque element in the blue ceiling, concealing a hatch that leads to the bell chamber.

CHURCH IN THE ROCK
The curved copper roof of Helsinki's Temppeliaukio church—known as the "Church in the Rock"—contributes to the excellent acoustics that make this a popular concert venue as well as a unique place of worship. The church, designed by Timo and Tuomo Suomalainen and completed in 1969, has been excavated from the granite bedrock.

The timber in the transversal naves lends a rustic feel to the church's atmosphere. The perfection of the simple but skilled and durable carpentry is clear in the joinery throughout the church. Shaded from sunlight and relatively unscarred by the other elements, the northern face of the church remains pure, untreated timber and has never been tarred, unlike the exposed southern face.

The carpenters of Finland's rural eighteenth- and nineteenth-century houses of worship would hardly recognize the more recent ecclesiastical creations as churches. In a church such as that at Myyrmäki in Vantaa, just to the north of Helsinki, traditional references are concealed within a less conventional, more eclectic framework. Even so, the architect of the church, Juha Leiviskä, sets great store by "the basic factors in architecture, the so-called eternal values," and insists that familiarity with tradition is an essential aspect of the architect's craft that encourages innovation rather than duplication.

The Myyrmäki church and parish center, conceived in collaboration with Pekka Kivisalo and completed in 1984, sits alongside many public buildings, including several churches, within Leiviskä's oeuvre. The Myyrmäki church demonstrates his conceptual approach: it follows a suburban railway track with a continuous white wall, while on the opposite side it traces a long, narrow arc. The white structure is matched by the slender silver birch trunks in the park on the side of the building away from the railway. A monolithic bell tower soars over the railway, while tall, narrow windows cast light into the upper reaches of the interior. Rather than intruding in shafts, the natural light is reflected through the space, and low-hanging lamps supplement the lighting. Wooden paneling enhances the acoustic qualities, underscoring the majestic roar from one of Finland's biggest organs.

Leiviskä has also talked of how a building can only be judged as architecture in terms of its context and setting and how it is affected by—and affects—the light that plays on its surfaces. Architecture, he argues, is an organic art form that has as much in common with music as it does with painting. In this sense, the distinctive and recognizable nature of his designs can be seen to follow a thread that links the continuing development of church architecture in Finland from the past and into the future.

KERIMÄKI

Although the startling size of the church at Kerimäki (above and facing page) in eastern Finland is often assumed to be the result of a building error, the lofty ceilings and generous space were part of a shrewd but simple intent to expand the congregation. Classical columns (facing page: top) inside sit surprisingly comfortably with the Gothic arch of the window. The church was a triumph of local craftsmanship: every man between the ages of fifteen and sixty was required to contribute to its construction, which was carried out under the supervision of one Axel Magnus Tolpo and, after his death, his son Theodor, in just three years.

FINNISH DESIGN
FOLLOWS A TRADITIONAL THREAD

A strong thread of design tradition connects the foundation of the Finnish Society of Crafts and Design in 1875 and the early art nouveau expressions of rising late nineteenth-century nationalism with the conspicuous modern Finnish design classics, which include Marimekko textiles, Stefan Lindfors interiors and furniture, the Globe, Bubble, Pastille and Tomato chairs of Eero Aarnio, Iittala glassware, and Fiskars tools and scissors. Finnish designers have also often taken a broad approach, in many cases regarding the discipline of design as a facet of a wider art. This is apparent in the fact that an architect such as Alvar Aalto can also be the creative force behind iconic design items like the bentwood chair and the Savoy vase. Eero Saarinen was likewise the designer of prize-winning 1940s furniture as well as the monumental TWA terminal at New York's JFK Airport.

Architect, designer, and writer Juhani Pallasmaa sees the Finnish design tradition as sharing the roots of the country's regard for architecture. "I would say that the quality of the best Finnish design arises from the same sources as the best architecture. There is a Finnish sensitivity towards objects. Moreover, in the more limited living conditions to which Finns have been accustomed, everything has value. I think Finns have developed a sense of value and sensitivity to things, as opposed to inhabiting a world of abundance where nothing has value."

Pallasmaa's own lengthy résumé, including the enormous new Kamppi Center rising in the heart of Helsinki, reflects an obsessive immersion in artistic creation of different kinds—not only of the

DESIGN CLASSICS
The birch wood sauna stool by Antti Nurmesniemi (left) was conceived for the Hotel Palace in Helsinki in 1951, and has survived and prospered as a Finnish design classic. The ceramic dishes (facing page) by Anneli Sainio, who is one of many artists with studios at Fiskars, won her the prestigious Kaj Franck Design Award in 2002.

buildings for which he is best known. He regards this kind of versatility as being practically encoded in the Finnish psyche, the rural, even pantheistic influences of which in his view remain powerful. "As for myself, I make no distinction between the things I do: writing, design, architecture," he says. "If I remember my childhood experiences in the early 40s, when I grew up on a Finnish farm, I never heard anyone ask: 'Can you do this?' It was taken for granted that you could do things. My grandfather could build sledges, tools, whole houses, and he could cure children and animals. Everything was related in that kind of farm life. The only real professions were the priest and the blacksmith."

The intimacy of Finland's social context is another explanation, he thinks, for the broad view of the Finnish designer, in addition to the social value projected onto the professions of design, architecture, and other creative activities. "It is more natural for we architects to design chairs and tables, for example, whereas in the USA the social and economic structures make it more difficult." A Finnish architect, in other words, need not be restricted to the planning of buildings, and his or her views on how those buildings may be used or filled can be more happily expressed and keenly heeded.

Juhani Pallasmaa describes Saarinen and Aalto as "strong figures occupying our mental lives in terms of setting examples. The greatest gift young people can receive is to be accepted into a profession, to feel comfortable." He attaches great importance to the tradition of Finnish design and the reference point it provides for a continuing and healthy interest in the skills of industrial arts and design. Genuine radicalism, he concludes, arises from familiarity with tradition.

Such a conviction tends to be confirmed by the work of a designer like Ristomatti Ratia, whose mother, Armi Ratia, was the founder of Marimekko. Ristomatti's work is a continuous exploration of new avenues, a refusal to be defined as the designer of any specific item or category, and an affirmation of versatility. His designs range from jewelry

PLAYFUL DESIGN
Facing page: The home of Eero Aarnio is bursting with playful furniture by this pioneer of creativity in plastic, from the Pony chairs in the foreground and the Parabel table (top), to the Screw table (bottom left), the hanging Bubble chair (bottom center), and the Ball chair (bottom right). Above: The glass of Oiva Toikka, displayed in an exhibition at Helsinki's Galerie Forsblom, includes the much-loved series of glass birds and eggs produced for Iittala.

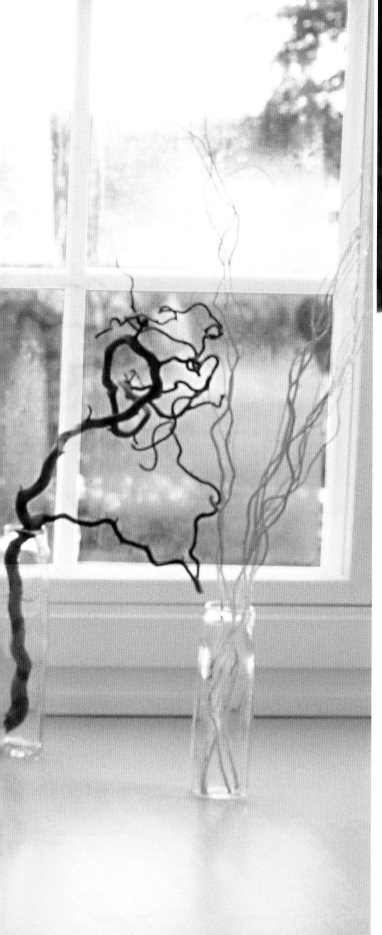

HOLISTIC DESIGN

Alvar Aalto's service trolley (left), designed for Artek, is a concise
demonstration of his belief in holistic design, where all the elements
of an object, a room, or a building complement one another.
The lantern on the trolley is by Harry Koskinen (left); the vases
(above) are by Ristomatti Ratia.

MOODS OF NATURE
Tonfisk Design's "Warm" range of cups and pots (above) are an innovative combination of wood and ceramics. Facing page: "All materials have their own unwritten laws": this declaration by designer Tapio Wirkkala (1915–1985) is manifested in his remarkable wood designs (top) and the classic glass creations (bottom) for which he is best known. The shapes of his glass art and tableware are evocative of the moods and movements of Finnish nature.

to glassware and from sauna stoves to bags, allowing him to develop an entire "Ratia Lifestyle" concept. Yet his philosophy remains true to the aims of simplicity and beauty pursued by his mother.

Paper yarn creations by Ritva Puotila represent the continuation of a similar tradition of stylish simplicity in Finnish design, and Puotila insists there is nothing gimmicky about her fondness for this most idiosyncratically Finnish of materials. As artistic director for the Woodnotes company, she has created a distinctive brand style that explores variations in the use of paper yarn, exploiting its attractive qualities and its functional strengths for their own value as much as for their novelty effect. Paper yarn is also surprisingly tough and durable.

Woodnotes has become Puotila's signature, but her career took a leap forward in 1960 when she won a Gold Medal at the XII Milan Triennale. She continued with a spell as designer for Dansk International, as well as freelance assignments in the Nordic region and the USA. She has experimented with the qualities of natural textiles, from silk and wool to cotton and linen, celebrating their properties and maintaining a suggestion of their natural origins. This approach is clearly visible in her Woodnotes collections, whose reedy tones and textures are evocative of the lakeshores and wind-frayed fields of her native country. "I wanted to produce a material and designs that were essentially Finnish," she explains.

All Woodnotes designs are made in Finland from the prime Finnish natural resource of renewable wood. They cover a surprising range of functions, from carpets and furnishing fabrics to blinds and table place mats, from bags and carriers to cushions.

The Woodnotes style is fresh and modern, yet remains firmly rooted in Finnish traditions of craft and innovation; it is one of the latest, finest demonstrations of the aesthetic and structural appeal of wood. From the intricate latticework of the Karelian villa to the perfect joinery of rural churches, saunas and sturdy, durable furniture, through to the deceptive delicacy of Woodnotes, the treasures of the forest are cherished.

SÁMI HANDICRAFTS

The far north of Finland, above the Arctic Circle, is the homeland of the Finnish Lapps, or Sámi, with their own languages and parliament, or Sámediggi. Within their language, the indigenous Sámi refer to duodji as the concept of expression through handicrafts and traditional arts (facing page and right). Although nowadays it employs only 10 percent of the Sámi, reindeer herding is symbolic of Sámi culture and reindeer skin is used for traditional shoes (right, top). Costumes and accessories, like those illustrated here from Utsjoki and Enontekiö, reflect local identities within the region. However, as Sámi women love to experiment with different fabrics and colors—not just the traditional red, yellow, blue, and green— this is a living and unusually flexible tradition.

References to the emblems and motifs of nature in the Finnish design of the last century amount to a consistent celebration of the natural environment. Tapio Wirkkala (1915–1985), called "a father figure of Finnish applied art" by his friend, colleague and fellow-designer Juhani Pallasmaa, was inspired by the shapes and textures of natural items, from seashells, birds, and fish to water in all its static, frozen, and flowing forms. Wirkkala was a versatile and prolific designer of everyday items of all shapes and sizes, including postage stamps, bank notes, and even ketchup bottles, but he is best known for his timeless glassware—notably the Ultima Thule range, whose rippled surfaces recreate the crystal ice of the Finnish winter, and his Chanterelle vases.

Following in the same tradition of visionary versatility is the industrial designer Timo Sarpaneva (born in 1926), who made his name—and Finland's—at the Milan Triennales of the 1950s. Sarpaneva's works—in glass, textiles, metal, and wood—reflect a pattern of Finnish sensitivity to light and an ambition to convey the beauty of the natural environment in everyday objects and utensils. Much of the impressive catalog of Finnish designers, through Kaj Franck to Antti and Vuokko Nurmesniemi and Oiva Toikka (celebrated for his decorative glass bird collections) demonstrate similar pioneering virtues.

Just as Wirkkala's and Sarpaneva's creations refuse to age, the instantly recognizable colorful "Unikko" poppy designs by Maija Isola of Marimekko's textile range have a fresh modernity that belies their thirty-year history. The showpiece Marimekko stores in Helsinki's stylish

EVERYDAY BEAUTY
Facing page: Simple, graceful, and sometimes whimsical shapes are characteristic of Finnish design, as is demonstrated in Inkeri Leivo's Gardena leaf bowl for Arabia; Kati Tuominen Niittylä's Grimmia platters and candleholders (top left); the wooden bowl by Petri Vainio for Artek (top right); ceramist Karin Widnäs's "baptism fountain" (bottom left); and Kati Tuominen Niittylä's very popular Storybird jugs (bottom right). Iittala's showroom display (left) includes Aalto glassware and the Gardena bowl.

LIVING CRAFT TRADITIONS
Traditional puukko knives (page 174), used by huntsmen and craftsmen, as well as treasured for their aesthetic quality, have been produced by Marttiini in Rovaniemi, the capital of Finnish Lapland, since 1928. The traditions of country crafts are expressed in a gentler way in the work of artist Markku Kosonen (page 175).

Esplanade are a rare magnet for both the design-conscious cognizant
and the casual gift hunter.

Although designs by Maija Isola—some drawing on original 1950s
and 1970s patterns (such as the 1976 Nile and 1952 Gates of Paris
compositions)—continue to evoke earlier styles while seeming to transcend the confines of period, the Marimekko umbrella also gives shelter to fresher talents. Recently these have included Maija Louekari and
Erja Hirvi. The international appeal of the Finnish approach was further confirmed in 2004 when the Victoria & Albert Museum in London
acquired the whimsical "Lehti" bowl by Marja Jauhiainen. Lehti (Leaf)
bowls are an ingenious metallic recreation of brittle fall leaves in brass,
sterling silver, and silver-plated brass, using unique processes to
achieve a superficial fragility that is deceptive.

Durability, continuity and—perhaps most crucially—unpretentious
popular appeal, rather than nostalgia, are the real keys to the success
of Finnish design. These qualities explain the resurgence in popularity
of the plastic furniture of Eero Aarnio; his creations are a refreshingly
mischievous departure from the rule whereby the motifs of nature are
clearly discernible in Finnish design. Pieces such as the hanging
Bubble chair, the Screw table, and the more recent Pony table take due
account of function, but their forms reflect the humor of their designer.

Perhaps the last word in Finnish design should go to Vuokko
Nurmesniemi, whose bright Marimekko striped textile designs—especially
the "Jokapoika" or "Every Boy" shirt—are as fresh today as when they first
appeared in the late 1950s. Together with her late husband Antti, Vuokko
adhered to the basic philosophy that "we have no right to produce rubbish.
Quality must be at the foundation of our designs." The simplicity and indi-
viduality of Finnish design are clear, she says, but "design belongs to the
world: it can make the difference between happiness and unhappiness."

HAIKKO MANOR

HAIKKO MANOR
*A south-facing patio is sheltered beneath classical columns
at the Haikko Manor (left) near Porvoo—a convenient
accommodation option for visitors to southern Finland
who want to stay near, but not in, Helsinki.*

HOTELS, RESTAURANTS, CAFÉS

"You have to be something special to be born twice." This was the slogan used for Helsinki's Hotel Kämp when it reopened its doors in 1999, referring to the fact that the hotel had been used as bank offices since 1965 and had undergone a complete reconstruction before its reincarnation. The hotel is named after its founder, the restaurateur Carl Kämp, who commissioned the architect Theodor Höijer to draw up plans for a major hotel in central Helsinki. The site chosen was the southern Esplanade Park, running down to the South Harbor, and now the location for most of Finland's main design stores.

The original Kämp opened in 1887 and became renowned as one of the most luxurious and prestigious establishments in the Nordic area. It also became something of a Finnish institution as the haunt of many high profile Finns. Finland's affection for the Kämp and the widespread delight at its reopening are in part due to its association with the last years of Russian rule and the burgeoning of independence. The chandeliers, classical columns, and ornate decorations of the Kämp—many of them faithfully brought back to life using archives and photographs—would have been familiar to the artist Akseli Gallen-Kallela and the composer Jean Sibelius. The poet Eino Leino (whose statue stands in the park outside) and statesman Marshal Mannerheim congregated here. The Kämp was also the meeting place for the Finnish nationalist Kagaali movement as Russian czarist rule drew to an end, and it served as a base for foreign journalists during the Winter War in 1939–1940.

HOTEL KÄMP
The Mannerheim Suite at the Hotel Kämp
(above and facing page), overlooking the Esplanade
park in the heart of Helsinki, represents the absolute
pinnacle of luxury in the Finnish capital.
Pages 182–183: The suites at the Hotel Grand Marina in
Helsinki extend to two floors, making imaginative use of
the space contained in the converted stores and warehouse.

As such, the Kämp holds a special place in the history of the Finnish people. It is also quite easily the most luxurious hotel in Finland. Its top-range clientele consists primarily of prestigious and top-flight business guests, as well as visiting entertainers and high-profile personalities. Yet in typically Finnish manner, it avoids overstepping the line into the territory of snobbish elitism.

There are 179 plush, elaborately decorated rooms, including Executive Rooms, Specialty Suites and the presidential Mannerheim Suite, and it is the style of presentation rather than the facilities themselves that sets the Hotel Kämp apart. From the original paintings by local artists to the fabric design, the ambience is ornate, a sophistication that reaches its pinnacle in the Mannerheim Suite. Here, late nineteenth-century references in the furniture and ornaments blend with the Italian marble of the bathroom and the spacious, modern design of the sauna.

This style strikes the guest from the moment of entry into the circular reception, where the light glints from an enormous chandelier. The library, a refuge of literary calm from the bustle of the Esplanade, is happily adjacent to the bar. In summer, a patio restaurant and terrace open from the bar onto the Esplanade, brushed by the evening sun—an interface between the ethereal opulence of the Kämp and the everyday life of the city.

The hotel's six second-floor function rooms pay due homage in their names to Finnish celebrities and earlier Kämp patrons: Aino Ackte, Akseli Gallen-Kallela, Eino Leino, Eliel Saarinen, and Jean Sibelius. The Conference Rooms, named after the Finnish Olympic running hero Paavo Nurmi, can seat 112, while the fabulous Mirror Hall is a sumptuous, glittering venue for balls and receptions.

The flamboyance of the Kämp, it must be admitted, is hardly representative of twenty-first-century Finnish accommodation, either in Helsinki or elsewhere in the country. Hotels are invariably comfortable and welcoming, but luxury in Finland is typically more restrained. Even so, imagination and innovation abound, as is evident in the renovation of Helsinki's Hotel Grand Marina.

The Rauhalinna Villa (facing page and right), built in the intricate Karelian style in eastern Finland in 1900 as a silver wedding present from a Czarist Russian officer to his wife, has a restaurant and a small summer hotel. In the same area is the Punkaharju State Hotel, close to the lakeshore and the pine-covered Punkaharju ridge, also dating from Czarist days and claiming to be the longest-established working hotel in Finland.

The possibility of converting the massive warehouse on the quay at Helsinki's South Harbor first dawned on its owners when it belonged to the Arctia chain at the end of the 1970s. The harbor was already in the process of changing from a cargo to an exclusive passenger and car terminal, and the warehouse found itself redundant in terms of its intended function. The building, constructed in three stages to the designs of Lars Sonck (1870-1956) in 1913, 1928, and 1930, is an especially impressive example of industrial architecture, with its 490-foot- (150-m-) long façade extending to seven floors. Sonck's other buildings include the gray finger of Helsinki's Kallio church and the city's Stock Exchange. The warehouse conversion was planned by the architects' office of Gullichsen-Kairamo-Vormala and completed in 1992, just in time for the follow-up talks for the Conference on Security and Cooperation in Europe, held that March in another converted warehouse located directly on the quayside.

The creation of charm and character from what was once a building of a more mundane nature has been achieved with great ingenuity. Air conditioning systems, stairs, and elevators, along with other technical functions, are enclosed in the central area of the hotel, making it possible for every room to have window access—no mean feat in a building that measures 160 feet (50 m) in width. There are a total of 462 rooms and sixteen different room types, with the highest commanding superb views across the South Harbor. These include twenty-eight suites on the sixth and seventh floors, some with split-levels to create a spacious apartment style.

The hotel boasts the longest sun-kissed bar and café terrace in summer, and has become well established as a favorite on the Helsinki hotel scene. Its location on the Katajanokka promontory, close to but at a comfortable distance from the main shopping and business centers and very near to the wonderful Jugendstil doorways and turrets of this district, is described by the management—at present the Scandic chain—as "five star." That such a robust and well-positioned building can be preserved and adapted to such admirable effect is a credit to the architects in particular and the city in general.

Innovative imagination has also been at work in the redevelopment of the erstwhile head office of a cooperative society into the SAS Radisson Plaza—an essay in clean, efficient, yet thoroughly relaxing, stylish Nordic comfort. Helsinki's range of hotels extends with each passing year, while the established favorites are refurbished with representative Finnish fervor. The Hotel Torni has recently reopened its doors to reveal updated interiors, while the Klaus Kurki has been undergoing a similar transformation.

Beyond the capital, similar comforts await the visitors to the provincial towns and cities, while the countryside occasionally offers accommodation in more traditional settings. Haikko Manor near Porvoo, for example, one of the country's favorite spa hotels, sits on a slope overlooking a scenic bay close to the mouth of the Porvoo river. The present manor—the design of Armas Lindgren, who also contributed to Helsinki's National Museum—dates to 1914, but there has been a manor of sorts here since the fifteenth century.

The manor at Mustio, also known by the dominant local Swedish-speaking community as Svartå, was completed in 1793 for Magnus Linder, owner of the ironworks that stood next to the Mustio river. Roughly equidistant between the southern cities of Helsinki and Turku, Mustio includes simple but charming lodgings in an exquisitely landscaped setting, surrounded by buildings of historical interest. The handsome yellow, three-story, all-wooden manor itself (which today belongs to a direct descendant of the original owner) stands as an elegant example of an architectural style that formed a bridge between the rococo and neoclassical styles. Designed by Turku architect Christoffer Friedrich Schröder and his Swedish colleague Erik Palmstedt, Mustio is one of the biggest wooden residential buildings in Finland, and rules over a cluster of historical outhouses and a small eighteenth-century church and bell tower close to the banks of the river. Through the mostly deciduous trees in the surrounding parkland, the buildings cast soothing reflections in a placid bay of the river.

A favorite venue for summer antiques fairs, the manor houses a museum, with sections available to rent for special functions. Guestrooms are distributed through the surrounding buildings and this is an ideal, isolated rural retreat for visitors intending to explore the attractions of southern Finland. No two guest rooms are alike, but all the rooms are well appointed, decorated in soft hues, and many look out onto the gardens.

HANKO VILLAS

Wooden villas, several housing cafés and guesthouses, grace the Baltic shoreline at Hanko, Finland's southernmost town. The House of the Four Winds Café (right) dates to 1910 and was later bought by Marshal Mannerheim to ensure privacy for his neighboring cottage. Hanko sits on a narrow peninsular and is an important port for cargo and passenger traffic whose proximity to the open sea makes it less restricted by ice in the winter months than the bigger harbor of Helsinki to the east, for example.

The Kappeli café and restaurant (far left) at the harbor end of Helsinki's Esplanade park is a city landmark and a popular meeting place, with a bustling outdoor terrace in summer. The magnificent granite entrance to the Hotel Lord (left) is typical of the Finnish National Romantic style, while the porch at the Tamminiemi Café (facing page) provides a relaxing shady retreat that retains the nineteenth-century character of its manor setting.

One of Mustio's claims to Finnish fame is that it boasts the first double-glazed windows in Finland, now regarded as essential minimum requirements in any construction. These were installed in the original building, along with what has remained as the country's oldest parquet floor in the study; the inlays are an intricate mosaic of walnut, birch, oak, and ash. Other special features include the magnificent tiled stoves in the Red and Yellow Salons; the latter, still in working order, is believed to be an authentic Swedish Marieberg stove. These stoves—a feature of Finnish and Swedish interiors—were an integral part of the heating system of the period, and many fine examples remain in Helsinki and Stockholm city apartments.

The interiors of the manor followed the favored Gustavian, or Louis XVI style. Another rarity for Finland in keeping with this style may be seen in the classical trompe l'oeil murals in the reception hall on the first floor. An original guest bed, thought to have been used by visiting czars and other dignitaries, remains in a guest room. An eleven-pound (5-kg) court uniform jacket, embroidered with gold-plated bronze thread and bearing the coat of arms of the last Russian czar, Nicholas II, is also on display.

Numerous portraits of previous occupants and visitors to the manor adorn the walls, including those of the iconic statesman and one-time president Marshal Mannerheim—who wooed the owner's daughter, Kitty Lander, only to be turned down on the grounds of dullness—and the extraordinary countess Marie Musina Pushkin.

Local historian Kirsten Ilander describes the countess as the "Lady Diana of her day": rich, beautiful, admired, but very unhappy. "People gossiped about her," says Kirsten Ilander. "She rode horses in the manner of men, not sidesaddle. She drank beer and smoked cigarettes and visited restaurants alone. She was also brave: in 1863 she approached the czar in Helsinki (Finland was at this time a Grand Duchy of the Russian Empire, under the Orthodox Church) and requested of him, directly, freedom of religion for Finland." The czar was stunned into silence, but Marie's wish was not granted until after her premature death at the age of thirty-nine.

The gardens today owe much to the English style preferred and nurtured by Fridolf Linder at the end of the 1860s. The waterside location provided a perfect setting for Linder's vision, since water was an important element of the English theme, and an exotic legacy remains in the shape of an Amur cork tree and some American walnuts. The deciduous trees provide a shady route to the water's edge, and to reach the banks one passes two neo-Gothic stable buildings, one now used as a company training center, the other converted into a restaurant and guestroom reception.

NAANTALI

After-sauna coffee is served on the deck of the Sunborn Yacht (right), a stylish floating annex to the Naantali Spa Hotel, where the archipelago views are part of the therapy. The small harbor town of Naantali, a bracing stroll away, is where to find the Restaurant Merisali (below), favored for its fish menu and live music, its harbor views, and the charm of its century-old wooden spa pavilion location.

The so-called "Bridge of Love" crosses to the Trycksbacka Park, with a replica of a "temple" gazebo at the top of the slope—an eccentric fairytale folly topped with tiny turrets. Nearby, a long wooden walkway leads across a water lily garden. Following the river bank, one arrives at a small dam or lock crossing the river, on the other side of which are some original workers' houses, the oldest dating to 1770, and the Orangery, housing a modest winter garden, two saunas, and a pair of guest suites.

Another manor, at Wiurila, a few miles to the west of the southern Finnish town of Salo, has a neoclassical majesty at odds with its rural isolation. The columns and arches of its façades are a conscious reference by their architect, C.L. Engel, to his grander work in Helsinki's mid-nineteenth-century Senate Square. Engel was commissioned by the Armfelt family to add his signature to the stables complex in 1845, adding to the neoclassical template of the main house. This had already been provided at the beginning of the nineteenth century by Carlos Bassin, whose legacy also includes the handsome pink stone manor of Korpo Gård in the Turku archipelago.

The present manager of the manor, Anne Marie Aminoff, is a descendent of Count Carl August Armfelt and has turned the estate into an attractive complex that incorporates a cozy hostel in the manor building, as well as restaurants, a museum of horse-drawn wagons and sleighs from the eighteenth century, and a boutique of local handicrafts. The expansive grounds have been sufficient to construct an eighteen-hole golf course and the stables continue to thrive in their originally intended function.

The columns, arches, and pleasing yellow of the paintwork at Wiurila and in Helsinki are all elements of a contemporary fashion that found its ultimate expression in the Russian city of Saint Petersburg, when Finland had been newly taken under the wing of the Russian imperial eagle. Under Russian Grand Duchy rule, Finland's Swedish-speaking aristocracy and ruling classes continued to prosper, and it was Count Carl August Armfelt who developed Wiurila into an almost self-sufficient industrial mini-state, complete with its own brickworks, sawmill, distillery, granary, dairy, and even its own brewery, the oldest in Finland. The manor is close to an inlet from the sea and exported its own products through a small fleet of its own vessels.

Helsinki has its share of well-located waterside cafés and restaurants. One with an especially interesting position is Oasis, constructed in 2000 directly on the quayside in the Hietalahdenranta area of the city. The restaurant looks out onto a calm, unruffled marina, on the opposite side of which prowl the cranes of the West Harbor and

the shipyard, until recently a continuous production line for some of the world's biggest and most luxurious cruise ships. The red brick of the converted Sinebrychoff brewery is nearby, while across the busy road behind the restaurant rise some new luxury apartments that count Formula One star Kimi Räikkönen among their residents.

The Hietalahti market square and hall—a magnet for hunters of antique and used-goods bargains—is also close, but it is the maritime reference that defines the long, sleek restaurant.

Oasis is the work of Juha Ilonen, and he chose steel as the dominant material in keeping with the lurking cranes and air of industry that dominates the shipyard and harbor milieu. Although a promenade separates the restaurant from the water, the long, narrow design of the building allows all diners to feel close to the calming pool. The generous, west-facing windows collect the evening sunlight in summer, and after sunset the reflections of the apartment lights across the bay create a crystal symmetry.

The restaurant backs onto a fuel station—also the work of Ilonen—with inverted roof slopes in a V-shape. An element of humor is added by the ship's funnel that rises at the entrance to the restaurant, partly encircled by an external spiral stairway that leads to a spacious and covered roof terrace. Steel—treated where necessary to ensure that it endures the exposure to the seaward aspect—is by far the dominant material, but there are warming elements of opal glass and translucent glass brick.

Inside, the visitor passes a small welcoming lounge of sofas and oriental cushions, before being seated by the high windows. A simple, graceful ambience is deliberately in keeping with a modern and successfully experimental cuisine that fuses Asian and Antipodean

OASIS
The elongated, narrow design of the Oasis restaurant in Helsinki means that all diners are able to enjoy the quayside view as well as benefiting from the bright southern aspect, especially on long, light summer evenings. Oasis is at the modern end, in terms of both décor and menu, of a colorful spectrum of restaurants in the Finnish capital.

ROOMS WITH A VIEW

Café Piper (left), one of many cafés, bars and restaurants at Helsinki's island fortress of Suomenlinna, offers excellent sea views from its terrace and the adjacent shade of Finland's oldest English-style garden. A cool elegance greets guests in the rooms of the refurbished Hotel Torni (facing page), a landmark in the heart of the capital (Torni means "tower"). The intimate bar and terrace at the top of the tower are famous for what is probably the best panoramic view of the city center.

elements, drawing on mainly Finnish ingredients, but featuring the occasional exotic surprise. Jouni Leino of the Avarte office designed the interior; he has preserved a sense of intimacy by using wide hanging shades, reminiscent of huge inverted umbrellas. The diner feels that he or she has a private view of the harbor and that this view is one-way, as if ensuring invisibility from the strollers and joggers who pass occasionally on the promenade.

Oasis is one especially interesting specimen of the Helsinki and Finnish dining scene, the scope of which is broadening almost daily in terms of the menus being offered and the sheer number of eateries. While Oasis sits at the modern end of the dining spectrum, more traditional venues continue to thrive. In Finland, the most convivial locations for dining are often those that are also appreciated as venues for sharing a beer or a bottle of wine. Helsinki "institutions" such as Elite and Kosmos are examples of this: while both offer excellent menus featuring the best of fresh Finnish cuisine, from forest berries and mushrooms to fish and game, their restrained hints of art nouveau provide the setting for relaxed and affable social gatherings. Finland's excellent indigenous culinary fare is also on offer at the finest gourmet establishments, including the Savoy, which has the added attraction of its elegant Alvar Aalto design.

Supplementing the restaurant scene, in Helsinki and further afield, is a generous selection of cafés that reflects the Finnish fondness for coffee and accompanying pastries and confectioneries. Establishments such as Café Succès and Café Esplanad, which share the same ownership, welcome a continuous throng of bustling tourists and locals in the capital, keen to sample the enormous cinnamon buns that are the specialty there. More graceful, less frenetic settings are supplied at the Tamminiemi and Villa Angelica cafés, both of which are housed in picturesque, antique-packed wooden houses close to the Seurasaari Open-Air Museum.

From the brisk modernity of Helsinki's hotels and the restrained historical charm of the manors of southern Finland, to the replenishing welcome of the capital's bars and cafés and the exquisite flavors of fresh and wholesome Finnish foods, visitors will be surprised and delighted at the range and quality of accommodation and dining options in what is, after all, one of Europe's most pleasantly surprising countries.

A Practical Guide

An insider's guide to the best addresses in Finland, including the favorite places to sleep, eat, drink, shop, and visit compiled by the author and the team that collaborated to produce this book.

It offers a subjective view of Finland's attractions and, while not exhaustive, lists personal choices alongside established classics.

The guide is organized into four sections: Helsinki, Southern Finland, The Lakes, and Northern Finland (Lapland). The emphasis, however, is on the attractions of Helsinki, the Finnish capital.

For the Helsinki section, hotels, restaurants, and museums are organized in alphabetical order, while the other sections are arranged alphabetically by city name.

Locations, phone numbers, Internet references, and e-mail addresses are included in the guide where possible. The international dialing code for Finland is 358, followed by the area code without the first zero, followed by the number. Opening times and prices change from season to season: we recommend that you confirm before booking.

TIMELESS APPEAL OF MARIMEKKO

Facing page: Ever since Jackie Kennedy appeared on the cover of Sports Illustrated in a Marimekko cotton print dress in 1960, the designs of this Finnish company have enjoyed global recognition and popularity. The poppy, or unikko, motif conceived by Maija Isola adorns a variety of products from duvet covers to mobile phone cases. The fact that it is even more popular today than when it first appeared in 1964 is conclusive proof that Finland's best design, with its uncomplicated but sophisticated appeal and quality, is capable of transcending the whims of fashion.

HELSINKI

HOTELS

Finland has an abundance of mid-range hotels up and down the country, along with some superb five-star establishments in the capital, Helsinki, and levels of cleanliness and efficiency are of the high standard expected throughout the Nordic countries. Breakfast is invariably included in the room price. Guesthouses offering bed and breakfast are few and far between and the concept as such is not well established in Finland. Summer farm accommodation, however, is an increasingly popular choice, especially for families. Holiday accommodation options also include privately rented self-catering cabins and chalets, often idyllically isolated by lakesides or on seashores. In our selection, we focus on hotels and guest accommodation in different parts of the country, especially those with a distinct and special character.

ACCOME SKATUDDEN (apartments)
Kauppiaankatu 5
00160 Helsinki
358 (0)9 2511 050
info.skatudden@accome.com

ACCOME TÖLÖ (apartments)
Museokatu 18 (Museigatan 18)
00100 Helsinki
358 (0)9 2511 050
info.tolo@accome.com

CROWNE PLAZA HELSINKI
Mannerheimintie 50
00260Helsinki
358 (0)9 25210000
helsinki.cph@restel.fi

Known for many years as the Hesperia, the Crowne Plaza reopened in spring 2005, promoting itself as a significant addition to Helsinki's business hotel scene. Rooms are state-of-the-art in terms of comfort and luxury amenities. Clubrooms and suites occupy the top floors, offering great views over the Hesperia park and across the Töölönlahti bay. All this, just five minutes by tram from the city center.

CUMULUS SEURAHUONE
Kaivokatu 12
00100 Helsinki
358 (0)9 691 41
Helsinki's quirky main Railway Station stands directly opposite the Seurahuone, and other attractions including the Museum of Contemporary Art are a few minutes away, making this an excellent location. Rooms are well soundproofed, allowing guests to leave the traffic behind. The circular bar, hidden below the reception, with a fountain in the center is worth a visit.

HILTON HELSINKI STRAND
John Stenbergin ranta 4
Helsinki
358 (0)9 39351
Located by the sea and close to a bridge leading west to the city center, the Strand has 192 newly renovated rooms and suites, and it prides itself on the Finnish design objects that decorate the rooms and corridors. The busy Hakaniemi Market Square and Hall are just behind the hotel, but accommodation here provides a restful haven.

HOTEL HILTON KALASTAJATORPPA
Kalastajatorpantie 1
00330 Helsinki
358 (0)9 45811
Kalastajatorppa—"fisherman's cottage"—has one of the best locations of all Helsinki's hotels. Surrounded by parkland, it sits on its own Baltic inlet, with sunset views that make it especially popular with honeymooners. The adjacent guesthouse has hosted various dignitaries, including President Reagan, who once slept here. Rooms are modern and spacious, and the hotel is some twenty minutes by tram from the city center.

KÄMP HOTEL
Pohjoisesplanadi 29
00100 Helsinki
358 (0)9 576 111
Simply unequalled in Finland in terms of luxury, elegance, and style, the Kämp stands on one side of the Esplanade park in the heart of town. First founded in 1887 and claiming a colorful history, the Kämp is something of a five-star legend. All 179 rooms—right up to the first class luxury Mannerheim Suite—are sumptuously decorated, butler service is available, and the bars and restaurants are among the most distinguished in town.

LORD HOTEL
Lonnrotinkatu 29
00180 Helsinki
358 (0)9 6158 1600
Set back from the bustle of the center yet within comfortable walking distance, the Lord Hotel's granite façade is typical of the Finnish national Romantic style from the beginning of the twentieth century.

The comfortable interior details are also representative of this style. Highly recommended for those seeking a combination of Nordic reliability and offbeat character.

PALACE HOTEL
Eteläranta 10
00130 Helsinki
358 (0)9 1345 6656
palacehotel@palace.fi
Classic hotel with a modern design and fabulous vistas over the harbor and the markets. Excellent gastronomic restaurant with a view and a lively, more casual restaurant—"Cocina"—featuring the cuisine of northern Spain.

RIVOLI JARDIN
Kasarmikatu 40
00130 Helsinki
358 (0)9 681 500
A small, independent hotel tucked away behind the Esplanade park and extremely handy for the top design shops, as well as the main Market Square, Market Hall, and South Harbor. The rooms are clean and airy, with more character than many slightly clinical Nordic hotel chain hotel rooms.

SAS RADISSON PLAZA
Mikonkatu 23
00100 Helsinki
358 (0)9 775 90
The Plaza is close to the main Railway Station in Helsinki, with the whole central area on its doorstep. The oldest parts of the hotel—including some impressive stained glass in the bar—are protected by order of the Helsinki City Museum. The older section also served as the head office for the SOK corporation, but the

conversion leaves little hint of this commercial past. Instead, the restaurant—named Pääkonttori, or "head office"—serves excellent European and Italian fare.

SCANDIC HOTEL GRAND MARINA

Katajanokanlaituri 7
00160 Helsinki
358 (0)9 16661
An ingeniously converted harbor warehouse on the Katajanokka promontory to the east of the city, the Grand Marina provides a handsome backdrop for the visiting cruise ships that dock here daily. First-class comfort has replaced the industrial function, and the two-story suites on the top floor offer harbor and rooftop views. The city center is a ten minutes' walk away or a couple of stops by tram.

SCANDIC HOTEL MARSKI

Mannerheimintie 10
00100 Helsinki
358 (0)9 68 061
www.scandic-hotels.fi/marski
marski@scandic-hotels.com
Comfortable centrally-located hotel close to all shopping facilities.

SCANDIC HOTEL SIMONKENTTÄ

Simonkatu 9
00100 Helsinki
358 (0)9 683 80
www.scandic-hotels.com
In the very heart of Helsinki, the elegant four-star Scandic Hotel Simonkenttä is an example of modern architecture and ecological design. The hotel has an attractive restaurant with a varied menu, as well as a summer terrace, sauna, and gym.

HELSINKI

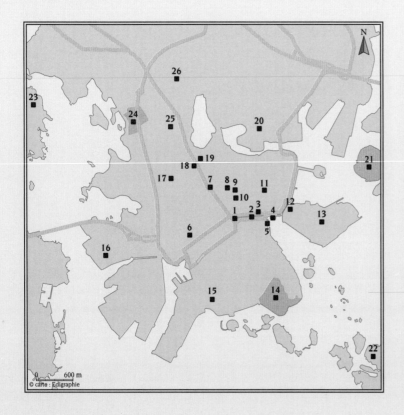

HELSINKI MAP KEY

1. Swedish Theater
2. Esplanade Park
3. Helsinki Tourism Office
4. Market Place
5. Wanta Kauppahalli market
6. Kamppi Center
7. Kiasma Museum of Contemporary Art
8. Railway Station
9. National Theater
10. Ateneum Art Museum
11. Senate Square and Cathedral
12. Uspenski Cathedral
13. Katajanokka
14. Kaivopuisto Park

15. Eira
16. Cable Factory
17. Temppeliaukio Church
18. Finnish Museum of Natural History
19. Finlandia Palace
20. Hakaniemi Market
21. Korkeasaari (The Helsinki Zoo)
22. Suomenlinna Fortress
23. Seurasaari Open-Air Museum
24. Sibelius Park and Monument
25. Töölö
26. Olympic Stadium

SOKOS HOTEL TORNI

Yrjonkatu 26
00100 Helsinki
358 (0)9 43360
Torni is one of the landmarks of central Helsinki; its name means "tower" and many of the rooms are located in this feature. The Ateljee bar at the top offers one of the best views of the city. The hotel itself reopened its doors in spring 2005 after extensive renovations, refining its restrained but distinctive National Romantic character.

SOKOS HOTEL VAAKUNA

Asema-aukio 2
00100 Helsinki
358 (0)9 43370
This monument to Functionalism was constructed in 1952 for the Helsinki Olympics. The hotel reception is on the ground floor, opposite the Railway Station, but most rooms are on the upper floors above the Sokos department store. The Loiste restaurant, which offers fine views across the city center, occupies the top floor.

RESTAURANTS

The Finns are great travelers, a fact reflected in the continuous evolution of Finland's restaurant scene into one that welcomes ethnic influences from all over the world. Chinese, Thai, Malaysian, Indian, Nepalese, Turkish, Greek, Italian, and Russian restaurants, to name just a few examples, are commonplace in the bigger towns and especially in Helsinki.
At the same time, the Finns have become more confident about the excellent culinary potential that

exists in Finland itself. Fresh Finnish ingredients are a match for those in any other country and they have their own distinct character. Freshwater and seawater fish of many different kinds—from salmon and Arctic char to vendace and perch—wonderful rye breads, mushrooms and berries, elk and grouse and other game, as well as reindeer are among the native ingredients, and more and more Finnish restaurants are promoting them on their menus. Some style themselves as Finnish restaurants per se, while others integrate the edible treasures of Finnish lakes and forests into international recipes with great success. Our selection introduces primarily those fine restaurants that are not afraid to make a meal of the best of Finnish ingredients. The line between bar and restaurant is sometimes a little blurred in Finland—at many of these places you can therefore simply enjoy a convivial beer or glass of wine.

BELLEVUE

Rahapajankatu 3
00160 Helsinki
358 (0)9 179 560
info@restaurantbellevue.com
In Soviet days, Helsinki was reputed to have the best Russian restaurants in the world. Restaurants in Russia have certainly caught up, but as the oldest of its kind in Finland (having opened in 1917, the year of Finland's independence), Bellevue retains a classical atmosphere and reputation for excellent food. The prices reflect the quality, and the chefs will prepare your favorite Russian dishes in the unlikely event of them not being on the menu.

CHEZ DOMINIQUE

Ludviginkatu 3-5
00130 Helsinki
358 (0)9 612 73 93
info@chezdominique.fi
Scandinavian gourmet cuisine is on offer at this restaurant, the proud and deserving winner of its second Guide Rouge star in 2003. High quality, from its ingredients to the tasteful décor, is the core principle, and the menu is devised by one of Finland's best-known chefs, Hans Välimäki.

DEMO

Uudenmaankatu 9-11
00130 Helsinki
358 (0)9 2289 0840
The Demo is hard to get to but worth the effort, with tasty cuisine made by a French chef. Small and atmospheric.

EST.1887

Pohjoisesplanadi 29
00100 Helsinki
358 (0)9 5761 1204
myyntipalvelu@royalravintolat.com
Est.1887 is the main restaurant at the opulent Kämp Hotel; the style of the marble columns and paintings, as well as the select menu, are in keeping with the quality of that establishment. In summer, pre- or post-dinner drinks can be enjoyed on the terrace on the Esplanade.

FISHMARKET

Pohjoisesplanadi 17
00170 Helsinki
358 (0)9 1345 6220
sales@palaceravintolat.com
FishMarket opened on the site of a long-established fish restaurant in 2004, with a fresh new modern interior and an imaginative menu that pays homage to Finland's seafood bounty. The restaurant is fittingly located just the length of a fishing line away from Helsinki's South Harbor and the fish stalls at the Market Square.

GEORGE

Kalevankatu 17
00100 Helsinki
358 (0)9 647662
www.george.fi
Closed Saturday lunch and Sundays. Boasting one Michelin star, the George was elected Restaurant of the Year 2004 for consistently excellent food, service, and atmosphere. The best fresh Finnish produce is deftly turned into delicate, tasty dishes by chef Markus Aremo, who favors the techniques of French cuisine. The set luncheon menu at nineteen Euros represents wonderful value for money. Dinner in the evening is a la carte.

G.W. SUNDMANS

Eteläranta 16
00130 Helsinki
358 (0)9 622 6410
myyntipalvelu@royalravintolat.com
Designed by C.L. Engel, the Empire style of the eponymous former home of a sea captain has been lovingly preserved at G.W. Sundmans, directly opposite the main Market Hall near Helsinki's South Harbor. However, diners are likely to be too absorbed in the sumptuous menu, which includes guinea fowl, Arctic char, and salmon, to appreciate the harbor view.

KATAJANOKAN KASINO

Laivastokatu 1
00160 Helsinki
358 (0)9 622 2722
Gambling no longer goes on at the old casino in Katajanokka, and the risk is small of receiving anything other than fine food and good service at this classic Helsinki restaurant, which also boasts a glorious summer terrace. The casino was constructed for officers of the Russian army when Finland was still a Grand Duchy of the Russian Empire in 1913, and retains a beguiling sense of history.

KOSMOS

Kalevankatu 3
Helsinki
358 (0)9 647 255
A favorite with artists and writers, privately-owned Kosmos has a lively buzz, and its hints of kitschy art nouveau and the giant potted plants lend a unique atmosphere. Book early to claim one of the intimate alcove tables. Also an animated spot for a drink for those who do not intend to dine.

KUU (MEANING "MOON")

Töölönkatu 27
00260 Helsinki
358 (0)9 2709 0973
In a quiet spot behind the Crowne Plaza, Kuu is an intimate local restaurant with fine wines and an excellent menu. Being a small place, it is worth booking in advance.

LAPPI – THE LAPP RESTAURANT

Annankatu 22
00100 Helsinki
358 (0)9 645 550
A recreation of a Lapp-style dwelling in the heart of Helsinki, Lappi serves all the classic dishes, from lean and nourishing reindeer stew with potatoes and lingonberries to grilled breast of snow grouse, Arctic char with cep mushrooms, and cloudberry desserts. The place to go to sample the most exotic ingredients that Finland has to offer.

LEHTOVAARA

Mechelininkatu 39
Helsinki
358 (0)9 440 833
Near the Sibelius Monument, Lehtovaara has offered seasonal food and a classic range of beef dishes for many decades. Quality is high and prices are reasonable. The glassed-in veranda is pleasant on a cool sunny day and the old-time waiters contribute to the family Sunday lunch atmosphere.

LYON

Mannerheimintie 56
00260 Helsinki
358 (0)9 408 131
marjatta.helander@lyon.inet.fi
Since first winning the Restaurant of the Year Award in 1996, Lyon has picked up several more prestigious prizes along the way. It is a cultured haven of calm that is a favorite with opera-goers (the National Opera is just across the road) and prides itself on using the very best fresh Finnish ingredients.

MAXILL

Korkeavuorenkatu 44
Helsinki
358 (0)9 638873
A trendy lively bar and restaurant in the pleasant shopping street of Korkeavuorenkatu. The food is good, the service efficient and friendly, and the atmosphere conducive to conversations with the locals.

HELSINKI

MECCA
Korkeavuorenkatu 34
00130 Helsinki
358 (0)9 1345 6200
A large, trendy place with nice food and atmosphere.

NJK
Valkosaari
00140 Helsinki
358 (0)9 639 261
Open only from May 1 to October 1. The NJK yacht club summer restaurant is located on its own splendidly isolated island just offshore of Helsinki's South Harbor; the cruise ships to Stockholm pass so close it almost feels as if you can reach out and touch them. The restaurant, reached only by a small shuttle ferry, is housed in a wooden villa dating from 1900. A superb setting for late summer crayfish parties.

NOKKA
Kanavaranta 7
00160 Helsinki
358 (0)9 687 7330
Nokka, in the row of converted red-brick storehouses running along the quay beneath the Uspenski Orthodox Cathedral, is a proud promoter of the best of Finnish food. Reindeer, game, fish, and the finest Finnish cheeses figure on the menu, and there is an excellent wine list. In summer, diners can enjoy a terrace on the quay.

OASIS
Hietalahdenranta 6
00120 Helsinki
358 (0)9 681 15 10
oasis@cafetering.fi
Architect Juha Ilonen has given this new building on the edge of Helsinki's western docklands the appearance of an ocean-going cruiser, complete with funnel. The length of the building ensures generous natural lighting for diners, who can enjoy an imaginative menu drawn from eclectic exotic sources (and sauces).

PALACE GOURMET
Eteläranta 10
00130 Helsinki
358 (0)9 1345 6715
sales@palaceravintolat.com
The Palace Gourmet is above the Palace Hotel, with brilliant views across the South Harbor, Retaining its original 1950s ambience, the kitchen nonetheless is bang up to date and features a seven-course Menu Surprise that changes from day to day. It also offers a wine list that runs to no fewer than four hundred titles.

RAVINTOLA ELITE
Eteläinen Hesperiankatu 22
00260 Helsinki
358 (0)9 434 2200
The name implies exclusiveness, but Elite welcomes all. Equally popular as a social meeting place or a dining spot (although its organic Finnish menu represents fine value for money), this Helsinki classic is a magnet for both refined artists, whose works decorate the walls, and for local residents.

RAVINTOLA HARITON
Kasarminkatu 44
Helsinki
358 (0)9 6221717
Delicious Russian food in a casual atmosphere. The best blinis in town with a variety to choose from in the February before Lent. Wonderful mushroom dishes from mushrooms picked by the monks of Hariton's Russian orthodox monastery outside Helsinki of which the restaurant is a sort of annex.

RAVINTOLA SAARI
Sirpalesaari
00150 Helsinki
358 (0)9 7425 5566
saari@arestaurants.com
Open only in summer.
To get there, catch the boat at the dock of the Karuselli café. Provides a truly unforgettable archipelago experience near the heart of Helsinki. Delicious herrings and archipelago bread and crayfish in season are served either in a cottage-like wooden house or, weather permitting, outside on the granite cliffs overlooking the Baltic.

RAVINTOLA SÄRKÄNLINNA
Särkänsaari
c/o Palace Ravintolat Oy
Eteläranta 10
00130 Helsinki
358 (0)9 1345 6756
sales@palaceravintolat.com
Särkänlinna, which is on a small island offshore from the Kaivopuisto park, is reached by a small ferry from the dock near Café Ursula in Kaivopuisto. The summer restaurant is housed in a nineteenth-century military fortification; the floor of the main dining room retains a very slight slope that was purposely designed so that gunners could roll their cannonballs from one end to the other. An archipelago menu with an excellent island view.

RAVINTOLA TEATTERI RESTAURANT
Pohjoisespa 2
00130 Helsinki
358 (0)9 681 1130
Teatteri Restaurant is also an eatery with an interesting design and upstairs discotheque. At the moment, a very trendy place late at night with a big bar inside.

SASSO RESTAURANT
Pohjoisesplanadi 17
00170 Helsinki
358 (0)9 1345 6240
sales@palaceravintolat.com
Recommended by the Laura Gutman LV guide, Sasso is an Italian and fish restaurant. Both designer establishments are located on the Esplanade. With a nice view over the harbor, Sasso has a modern decoration highly characteristic of Finland.

SAVOY RESTAURANT
Eteläesplanadi 14
00100 Helsinki
358 (0)9 684 4020
As well as boasting the 1930s design of Alvar Aalto, the Savoy, above the Esplanade park, has one of the best views in Helsinki and a special Savoy Menu that changes every day. Popular for high-powered business meetings, but also ideal for special occasions.

SEA HORSE
Kapteeninkatu 11
Helsinki
358 (0)9 628 169
Those who want to sample convivial, local dining and atmosphere in Helsinki could do no worse than try the fried herrings and mashed potato at Sea Horse. Nothing fancy here: just a simple menu offering ample portions and a friendly clientele.

STRINDBERG

Pohjoisesplanaadi 33
00100 Helsinki
358 (0)9 681 2030
A very popular luncheon spot in the middle of town with views to the Esplanade park. Just above the Café Strindberg, the restaurant offers an attractive luncheon menu, as well as such classics as Caesar Salad and home-cooked dishes including meatballs and Wallenberg steak. Reservation recommended.

VIA

Ludviginkatu 10
00130 Helsinki
358 (0)9 681 1370
A large, casual, and noisy "canteen" for the media people working in the area. Woks, wraps, and large natural wood tables, as well as a table d'hôte attract a large crowd.

WALHALLA

Suomenlinna A7
00190 Helsinki
358 (0)9 668 552
walhalla@kolumbus.fi
Walhalla has one of the most exciting and romantic locations of any restaurant in Helsinki. It stands in the ramparts of the island fortress of Suomenlinna, construction of which started in 1748 and as such is also one of the most historic parts of the capital. The candlelit restaurant, opened for the Olympics in 1952, is set in an atmospheric chamber of arched brickwork.

WELLAMO

Vyökatu 9
Helsinki
358 (0)9 663 139

A highly recommended "Gallery Restaurant," Wellamo is hidden behind a granite stairway on the northern side of the Katajanokka peninsular. Wellamo is the kind of small restaurant that Helsinki does best: unpretentious, unfussy, and uncomplicated but excellent food made from local fresh ingredients. Lamb soup, pickled cucumbers with honey and smetana, and flambéed green pepper strawberries are among the favorites. A small but discerning wine list, too.

CAFÉS AND BARS

The Finns love coffee, as visitors will deduce from the abundance of cafés in the capital. Many of these also function as lunchtime restaurants, serving hearty snacks and salads, while a select few are classic institutions, alluring passers-by with the warm aromas of fresh coffee and cinnamon rolls. The Finnish bar scene, meanwhile, continues to expand with every passing year and ranges from English and Irish style pubs, impressively-stocked wine bars, and thudding night clubs to no-nonsense gathering places for the local community. Age limits are enforced at some bars and door staff may request proof of age. Some of the restaurants mentioned above—for instance, Kosmos, Elite, and Sea Horse—also have bars that are popular with those who visit for a relaxed drink rather than a full-scale meal. Our guide suggests a cross-section of the most interesting and convivial cafés and bars in Helsinki.

ARCTIC ICE BAR

Located in the nightclub *Uniq Nightlife*
Yliopistonkatu 5
00100 Helsinki
www.uniq.fi

CAFÉ AALTO

at the Academic Bookshop
Pohjoisesplanadi 39
00101 HELSINKI
358 (0)9 121 41
Refreshments for browsers at Helsinki's best bookstore, designed by celebrated architect Alvar Aalto.

CAFÉ CHAPMAN

Suomenlinna B 1
00190 Helsinki
358 (0)9 668694
info@ravintolacafechapman.net
Open from May, Café Chapman provides a romantic refueling station for explorers of the Suomenlinna island fortress throughout the summer. It is housed in a fortification close to the bridge linking the two main islands of the fortress and overlooking the Tykistölahti inlet. Chapman serves a full lunch and dinner menu, as well as snacks and coffee.

CAFÉ EKBERG

Bulevardi 9
00120 Helsinki
358 (0)9 6811 8660
ekberg@cafeekberg.fi
Ekberg was founded in 1852 and hints of its history remain in the aprons of its waiting staff and the general air of elegance. Next door to the café in the central tree-lined Bulevardi is the equally elegant Ekberg patisserie shop.

CAFÉ ESPLANAD

Pohjoisesplanadi 37
00100 Helsinki
358 (0)9 665 496
info@esplanad.fi
The big cousin of Café Succès, the recently enlarged Café Esplanad is on the Esplanade park and is a lunchtime magnet. The same enormous buns, snacks, and sandwiches as in Café Succès are on sale here, but cheerful bustle is the attraction at the Esplanad rather than quiet intimacy.

CAFÉ KARUSELLI

Merisatamanranta 10
00150 Helsinki
358 (0)9 622 4522
This café is a must in spring and summer although open year round (10 A.M.–7 P.M.). Serves as a light lunch place with large sunny terrace for watching people and boats go by (see Ravintola Saari on island opposite). The interior architecture is exciting.

CAFÉ MUTTERI

Lauttasaarentie 2
00200 Helsinki
358 (0)9 670 046
Between the two larger sisters mentioned above is a small café-kiosk with a few tables and chairs and piles of blankets for enjoying the first rays of sunshine in the spring and throughout the summer months. Tiny but sweet.

CAFÉ SUCCÈS

Korkeavuorenkatu 2
00140 Helsinki
358 (0)9 633 414
info@succes.fi
Sampling the enormous, fresh cinnamon buns known in Finnish as

HELSINKI

korvapuusti, or "a slap round the ear" at Café Succès is an essential Helsinki experience. The café is cozy and very popular—well worth the short wait that may be necessary on brisk Sunday afternoons.

CAFÉ TIN TIN TANGO
Töölöntorinkatu 7
00260 Helsinki
358 (0)9 2709 0972
Tin Tin Tango bills itself as a "truly European style" café, but only in Finland would you find a sauna (advanced booking required) and a launderette at the back. As if this were not enough, the café has its own bakery and its walls also serve as a gallery for local artists. Fun and friendly.

CAFÉ URSULA
Ehrenströmintie 3
00140 Helsinki
358 (0)9 652 817
cafe.ursula@columbus.fi
This café is a Helsinki institution. Open year round, it is one of the few establishments right by the sea where one can sit and admire the seascape and meet friends after a walk along the shore or through Kaivopuisto. Always a very popular venue.

CORONA BAR
Eerikinkatu 11
00100 Helsinki
358 (0)9 642 002
Corona is a favorite pool and snooker bar and sits above the Andorra movie theater founded by film directors, the Kaurismäki brothers. Lively, hip, and happy.

ENOTECA WINE BAR
Ludviginkatu 8-10
00130 Helsinki
358 (0)9 681 1370

Enoteca is housed in the former Helsingin Sanomat newspaper offices in Ludviginkatu and has an Italian produce shop next door. A superb choice of wines and a whimsically classical ambience, assisted by the dark brown wooden ceiling.

JASKAN GRILLI near the **Storyville jazz club** (excellent) serves up hearty grilled sausage with all the trimmings (the Finnish nighttime reveler's snack par excellence) to offset any dawn hunger pangs after a night on the town.

JUTTUTUPA
Säästöpankinranta 6
00530 Helsinki
358 (0)9 7744 860
marcopolo@juttutupa.com
Juttutupa is located in a magnificent granite castle of a building close to an inlet from the sea. There are no outward signs of its traditional association with socialist causes: sociability, however, is a dominating theme in this atmospheric, down-to earth-establishment. Wednesday nights are live jazz nights.

KÄMP BAR
Hotel Kämp
Pohjoisesplanadi 29
00100 Helsinki
358 (0)9 576 111
The most elegant and expensive bar in Helsinki, but a good place to spot local and visiting celebrities over a perfectly served cocktail.

KAPPELI BAR CAFÉ
Eteläesplanadi 1
00130 Helsinki
358 (0)9 681 2440

kappeli@sok.fi
The Kappeli pavilion at the harbor-end of the Esplanade park is one of Helsinki's central landmarks and favorite meeting spots. The expansive summer terrace faces a bandstand for evening entertainment, and visitors can choose between a beer, coffee, and snack in the café and basement bar or a full meal in the adjacent restaurant.

KUU KUU
Museokatu 17
00100 Helsinki
358 (0)9 2709 0974
The art that adorns the walls is a clue to the clientele at this favorite Helsinki haunt of artists and cultural personalities, which is also popular with late-night weekend partiers.

O'MALLEYS PUB
Yrjönkatu 28
00100 Helsinki
358 (0)9 4336 6330
The Irish bar at the recently refurbished and renovated Torni Hotel, O'Malleys remains the best of the Irish bunch in Helsinki. A long-time favorite with ex-pats and locals alike, it boasts a cozy sheltered patio in summer and live music in the bar.

PULLMAN BAR
Rautatieasema
00100 Helsinki
358 (0)9 0307 22930
pullmanbar@avecra.fi
Wait for your train or bus with a beer or one of the fine malt whiskeys at the Pullman Bar, above the Eliel restaurant at Helsinki's main Railway Station.

Journalists with press cards can use the Press Club behind the whiskey bar. Interiors here, with strong hints of National Romantic, are the work of Eliel Saarinen.

RAVINTOLA KAIVOHUONE
Iso Puistoli 1
00140 Helsinki
359 (0)9 621 2160
info@ravintolakaivohuone.fi

STORYVILLE JAZZ CLUB
Museokatu 8
Helsinki
358 (0)9 408 007
www.storyville.fi

STUDIO 51
Fredrikinkatu 51-53
00100 Helsinki
358 (0)9 612 9900
info@studio51.fi
Studio 51 is the stylish club of choice for the older set, while **Kaivohuone** in the center of Kaivopuisto attracts the lively, trendy younger generation.

TAMMINIEMI CAFÉ AND VILLA ANGELICA
Tamminiementie 8
00250 Helsinki
358 (0)9 481 003
Both of these charming old-world cafés are near the causeway leading across to the Seurasaari Open Air Museum. Both are housed in wooden villas fitted out with antiques and offer outdoor garden seating in the summer. The former home (now a museum) of the late president Kekkonen and a branch of the Helsinki City Art Museum are also nearby.

TEATTERI

Pohjoisesplanadi 2
00130 Helsinki
358 (0)9 681 11 30
ari.tuoreniemi@royalravintolat.com
Sleek, clean lines and light flooding in from the terrace at the end of the Esplanade park make Teatteri, at the back of the Swedish Theater, a lively haunt.

TEERENPELI

Vuorikatu 16
00100 Helsinki
358 (0)9 424 925 200
www.teerenpeli.com
Teerenpeli sells a range of beers made in its own brewery. It also has branches in Lahti (where the brewery is located) and Tampere. This is a welcome, relaxed addition to Helsinki's nightlife options, and the friendliness of the staff helps to make it popular with different age groups. Also sells the biggest sandwiches in town.

TORI

Punavuorenkatu 2
00120 Helsinki
358 (0)9 6874 3790
Trendy, but with no airs or graces, Tori is a bright and breezy bar in the Punavuori area that also serves good quality, hearty meals.

SHOPPING

Our guide concentrates on shopping in the capital area, although various stores mentioned here have branches in the provinces, and small gift shops are dotted throughout the country. Local specialties, such as goods made from reindeer hide hailing from far northern Lapland, are widely available in Helsinki, too. Shopping in Helsinki, compared with the same activity in Europe's bigger metropolises, is pleasantly unrushed and stores are rarely overcrowded. Most of the major outlets are also comfortably located within walking distance of each other. The shop clerks are normally courteous and helpful, and most are willing and able to speak English. Prices for quality goods, such as designer glassware, may be somewhat higher in Finland than elsewhere in Europe, but bargains can be hunted down.

Finland, especially the Helsinki area, is full of large shopping malls where the visitor will find branches of the main national chains. The Jumbo shopping center, close to the Helsinki-Vantaa airport, is one huge example; Itäkeskus in eastern Helsinki is another.

• Department stores:

SOKOS

Mannerheimintie 9
00100 Helsinki
358 (0)9 765 000
helsinki@sokos.fi
Sokos is Stockmann's main department store rival in Helsinki. Its flagship store, a Functionalist masterpiece from the 1950s, is close to the main Railway Station. Prices at Sokos, which is the retail wing of the SOK cooperative, tend to be somewhat lower than those at Stockmann, and the Sokos stores scattered through the country outnumber those operated by Stockmann. Sokos offers a wide range of goods, from clothing to kitchenware and most items in between.

SWEAT IT OUT

The word **sauna** is the only word in the Finnish language that has become established in global parlance. Saunas are everywhere in Helsinki and the rest of Finland, in private homes and vacation residences, in hotels, health clubs, and swimming pools. The Finns are often fairly insistent that their guests sample this ritual. It is not regarded as bad manners to refuse, but the experience is often more pleasant than visitors anticipate.

The sauna is basically a closed chamber with wooden benches and a pile of stones assembled on top of a stove, onto which water is sprinkled to generate steam. This in turn causes the naked bather to perspire, a process that is considered to be therapeutic and restorative. The wood-burning sauna—of the kind nearly always found at lakeside summer homes—is considered to be preferable to the electrically heated variety, which is nonetheless widespread. Bathing is preceded and followed by a cooling dip in a lake or in the sea, and in the winter this practice is continued by dipping in a hole in the ice: more invigorating and enjoyable than one might imagine. Public saunas are either provided separately for men and women or have times reserved for male and female bathing.

The thousands of summer cottages and log cabins on Finland's sea and lakes are the best places to sample the sauna, but there are some options in Helsinki. The **Kotiharjun sauna** near the Sörnäinen Metro station (Harjuntorinkatu, tel. 09 735 1535) is a wood-heated city sauna: very rare in modern times. The **Finnish Sauna Society** at Vaskiniemi on the island of Lauttasaari to the west of Helsinki has two traditional smoke saunas, and there is a jetty from which visitors can try the *avanto* ("hole in the ice") option. One must be a member or guest of a member to bathe here, but holders of the Helsinki Card can book in advance by calling 09 686 0560 or 09 6860 5622. The columns and lofty ceiling of the **Yrjönkatu swimming hall** (Yrjönkatu 21, tel. 09 3108 7401) are reminiscent of a classical Roman spa: naked swimming after the sauna is standard here, with strictly observed separate times for men and women.

At Muurame, just over nine miles (15 km) to the south of the city of Jyväskylä, is a sauna village that has preserved about thirty smoke saunas (where bathers traditionally immerse themselves in sooty smoke before scrubbing themselves in snow or lake water), some of which are in working order. The sauna village is open only from June to August.

HELSINKI

STOCKMANN
Keskuskatu
00100 Helsinki
358 (0)9 121 51
www.stockmann.fi
Stockmann is a Finnish institution, as crucial a part of the picture of Helsinki life as Macy's in New York or Harrods in London. The flagship store occupies an entire block between the main shopping streets of Mannerheimintie, Keskuskatu, and Aleksanterinkatu, and the Academic Bookstore sits on the corner of the Esplanade and Keskuskatu. If you choose, you can do all your gift shopping at Stockmann, since the work of every important designer and design company, from Marimekko textiles to Wirkkala Ultima Thule glassware, is showcased here. Finnish delicacies are available in the food hall in the basement. Stockmann has branches in the Tapiola and Itäkeskus suburbs, as well as in the cities of Turku and Tampere, Moscow in Russia, Tallinn in Estonia, and Riga in Latvia. Stockmann also has a branch at Helsinki-Vantaa airport for last-minute gift shopping.

• **Books and music:**

The Finns are one of the best-read nations on the planet, yet the majority of sales—certainly of foreign language books, magazines, and newspapers—are handled by two dominant outlets.

The first is the **STOCKMANN ACADEMIC BOOKSTORE**, whose main store is on the corner of Keskuskatu and the Esplanade park (tel. 09 121 4243), but which also has branches in the Tapiola and Itäkeskus suburbs, as well as in Tampere and Turku.

The second is **SUOMALAINEN KIRJAKAUPPA** ("Finnish bookshop" tel. 09 852 751/09 696 2240), with a main store at Aleksanterinkatu 23 and branches scattered through the suburbs and other Finnish provinces. Both shops have good selections of foreign-language books (especially English) and foreign press, including an impressive range of daily newspapers from around Europe.

For music, visit the CD department in the basement at Helsinki's main Stockmann store. Work by Finland's remarkable pool of classical musicians can be purchased at **FUGA** at Kaisaniemenkatu 7. The best-stocked jazz and World Music shop in Finland is **DIGELIUS** (www.digelius.com) at Laivurinne 2, with a very well informed and enthusiastic staff.

For the little ones, do not miss the shop devoted to the **Moomins**, offering tasteful books and toys based on the characters of Tove Jansson in the Kämp galleria (Mikonkatu 9, 00100 Helsinki).

• **Clothing and footwear:**

ANNE LINNONMAA
www.annelinnonmaa.fi
Euro-ecological fashion for multiple wear. Visit the website for a list of stores.

HANNA SARÉN
Ultimate Design Oy
Tehtaankatu 27-29 D52
00150 Helsinki
358 (0)9 6124 1595
www.hannasaren.com
Hanna Sarén is also a leading show designer.

JUHA TARSALA is Finland's Manolo Blahnik of *Sex in the City* fame and has a tiny boutique in the Kämp Gallery (358 (0)9 681 34370).

MARIMEKKO is perhaps Finland's best known and most distinctive fashion house, offering a riotously colorful selection of fabrics, garments, bags, and table items. The classic poppy designs look as fresh today as they did three decades ago. Helsinki stores at Eteläesplanadi 14 (tel. 09 170 704) and Pohjoisesplanadi 2 (tel. 09 622 2317) and Pohjoisesplanadi 31 (tel. 09 686 0240).

PERTTI PALMROTH
(Aleksanterinkatu 26 and Pohjoisesplanadi 37). Stylish and fashionable footwear.

STOCKMANN (see above: "Books and Music") is a good bet for Finnish and international fashions under a single roof.
ALEKSANTERINKATU, known locally as **Aleksi**, is lined with various clothes shops, as is the Esplanade park, where **ANNIKKI KARVINEN** (tel. 09 6811 7513) fashions, for example, is to be found.

• **Jewelry:**

JAANA LEHTINEN: ROYAL PRINCESS DESIGN-ATELIER OY
Korkeavuorenkatu 2bF 70
00140 Helsinki

Jaana Lehtinen, on Museokatu, is the up-and-coming designer of more rock and roll jewelry.

KALEVALA KORU
Kalevala Koru jewelry—clasps, brooches, earrings, rings, bracelets, and necklaces—has an attractive and distinctively mythic Finnish theme and is named after *The Kalevala*, the Finnish national epic. The main store in the capital is at Unioninkatu 25 near the Senate Square (tel. 09 686 0400) with a factory shop at Strömbergintie 4.

TORBJÖRN TILLANDER
Oy Kluuvikatu 1
00100 Helsinki
www.tillander.com
Two sisters and topnotch gemologists apply their talents to create modern, wearable, and highly stylish rings, bracelets, and other accessories. They also design to order.

• **Finnish design kitchenware, traditional textiles, and gifts:**

AARIKKA (wooden gifts and jewelry, tel. 09 770 440/09 652 277) has stores on each side. **ARTEK** is the company set up by Alvar Aalto as a showcase for his design philosophies, and it has a thriving store on the south side, with furniture, fabrics, and tableware (tel. 09 6132 5277).

AERO DESIGN FURNITURE
Twentieth-Century Objects
Yrjönkatu 8
00120 Helsinki
358 (0)9 680 2185
www.aerodesignfurniture.fi
A wonderful place for modern

furniture, offering works by Eero Aarnio along with vintage signed pieces from Tapio Wirkkala, Gunnel Nyman, Alvar Aalto, and other Finnish design greats.

The shop at **DESIGN FORUM FINLAND** has moved to new Helsinki premises at Erottojankatu 7, 00130 Helsinki (www.designforum.fi; tel. 09 6220 810, info@designforum.fi). This is an excellent venue for gift shopping and sells items designed by the cream of Finnish design, from Antti Nurmesniemi to Kaj Franck. Wood, glass, steel, textiles, ceramics, and jewelry are all included in the selection.
Both the southern and especially the northern (Pohjoisesplanadi) sides of the long narrow Esplanade park are blessed with the top Finnish design shops.

DESIGNOR now named **IITTALA SHOP** (beautiful quality glass, kitchenware, and ceramics by Arabia, Hackman, Iitala, and Rörstrand) has a store on the north side. The Designor brands, as well as Pentik gifts and kitchenware and Marimekko textiles, are also to be found at the **ARABIA CENTER** (Arabiakeskus) at Hämeentie 135 (a twenty-minute number 6 tram ride from the city center). The Arabia Center was originally the factory shop of Arabia ceramics and is a great venue for gift and practical souvenir shopping, often at discount prices.
To get to the Arabia/Iittala outlet shop in Arabianranta, catch the designated bus at Kauppatori.

Traditional *ryijy* rugs are the specialty at **FRIENDS OF FINNISH HANDICRAFTS** at Runeberginkatu 40 (tel. 09 612 6050), and also at **WALLRUGS** at Abrahaminkatu 7 (tel. 09 6216 615). The **KISELEFF HOUSE**, in the Senate Square, contains many small craft and gift shops, including the **LITTLE RUSSIA** shops for icons and painted lacquered boxes from Finland's eastern neighbor, and toys and decorations from **FANNY AND ALEXANDER**.

GALLERIA NORSU
Kaisaniemenkatu 9
00170 Helsinki
A brand-new design exhibition space and shop for Fiskars handicraft artists.

HARRI KOSKINEN
www.harrikoskinen.com
A new designer, also working for Iittala.

Traditional *puukko* Finnish knives are beautifully crafted in Lapland and sold in Helsinki by **MARTTIINI** at Aleksanterinkatu 28 (tel. 09 633 207; www.marttiini.fi). These knives, which make beautiful gifts, can be decorative or actually used in the backwoods and hunting applications for which they were designed.

• **Antiques and fine arts:**

CLASSIC at Mariankatu 26 (tel. 09 455 3936) is one of several good antique shops in the Kruunuhaka area of Helsinki.
Finland's foremost fine art and antiques auctioneer is **HAGELSTAM** (Bulevardi 9A, 00120 Helsinki;

tel. 096877990; www.hagelstam.fi). Hagelstam buys and sells some six thousand items annually at its eight auctions, with Finnish, Swedish, and Russian art accounting for the majority of sales. Silver from the eighteenth and nineteenth centuries is another specialty.
Finland's obsession with everything new and modern finds an antidote in Helsinki at **TOMORROW'S ANTIQUE** (Hietalahdenranta 11, tel. 050 64 20: www.tomorrowsantique.com), which is by appointment only and specializes in Finnish design items and lighting from 1930 to 1970 by Aalto, Aarnio, Tappiovaara, Saarinen, and Wirkkala, to name but a few.

• **Fresh food:**

Most Finnish towns of any size have market halls and squares which are excellent sources of fresh Finnish foods, including (according to season) berries, mushrooms, fish, and bread. Market halls in Turku and Kuopio, for example, are especially colorful. The main **Market Square and Hall** in Helsinki, near the South Harbor, are marvelous and vibrant, especially in the summer, when a visit is one of the city's prime attractions. This is also where the annual Herring Fair is held in the first week of October, a vivid congregation of farmers and fishermen from the outlying archipelago. The **Market Square and Hall** at Hakaniemi, to the east of central Helsinki, has a more local flavor and is also well worth a visit.

The food hall at the main Stockmann store in Helsinki offers an excellent choice of fresh and packaged Finnish foods.

MUSEUMS, GALLERIES

Helsinki has many small private galleries in addition to the main art museums listed here. The rest of Finland is full of excellent art museums and cultural centers. We present here only a selection of some of the best loved and most popular.
Note that many museums in Finland are closed on Mondays and that some in the more remote districts are open only during the summer months.

AMOS ANDERSON ART MUSEUM
Yrjönkatu 27
00100 Helsinki
358 (0)9 6844 460
www.amosanderson.fi
museum@amosanderson.fi
Founded by the eponymous local printing magnate and opened in 1965 in his former home, this is one of Finland's biggest private art collections, embracing sculpture by Felix Nylund and paintings by Magnus Enckell and A.W. Finch. Amos Anderson is best known for its extremely popular changing exhibitions.

ART MUSEUM OF THE ATENEUM
Kaivokatu 2
00100 Helsinki
358 (0)9 173361
www.ateneum.fi
Inaugurated in 1887 and occupying one side of Helsinki's Railway Station Square, the Ateneum

contains the biggest collection of art in Finland, namely those works belonging to the Finnish National Gallery that cover the period from the mid-eighteenth century to the 1960s. Most of the collections represent Finnish art—including Albert Edelfelt, Hugo Simberg, Helene Schjerfbeck, and Aleksi Gallen-Kallela—but there is also a significant international collection that includes works by Cezanne, Chagall, Gauguin, Van Gogh, Munch, and Rodin. The Ateneum holds changing exhibitions that attract large and enthusiastic audiences, and has a pleasant café and a gift shop.

CABLE FACTORY

Tallberginkatu 1 C 15
00180 Helsinki
358 (0)9 4763 8300
www.kaapelitehdas.fi
This enormous former industrial complex on the edge of the Ruoholahti development district has been taken over by Helsinki's vibrant artistic community and houses exhibition and concert space, studios, dance theaters, photo galleries, and restaurants.

The **CITY OF HELSINKI MUSEUM** is distributed at various locations: visit the website at www.hel.fi/kaumuseo/english/index.html for information about changing exhibitions and opening times. The **Hakasalmi Villa** branch is opposite the National Museum and adjacent to the Finlandia Hall on Mannerheimintie in an attractive pink mansion (Karamzininkatu 2; tel. 09 169 3444). The villa hosts changing exhibitions, combining works of art and historical exhibits.

Other branches of the City Museum include the under-rated **Tram Museum**, a little further north along Mannerheimintie at Töölönkatu 51A (tel. 09 169 3576), with a history of Helsinki's public transport. It is housed in the city's oldest tram shed dating from 1900, part of which was used as stables for the horses that pulled the earliest trams. Another department of the museum is the **Burgher's House**, Helsinki's oldest wooden house, at Kristianinkatu 12 (tel. 09 135 1065), which was built in 1818 and is furnished and fitted in the style of a middle-class family residence from the 1860s.

DIDRICHSEN ART AND CULTURAL MUSEUM

Kuusilahdenkuja 1
00340 Helsinki
358 (0)9 4778 330
www.didrichsenmuseum.fioffice@didrichsenmuseum.fi
Housed in a modern villa shaded by woodland, this private museum, created by Marie-Louise and Gunnar Didrichsen, brings together twentieth-century Finnish art—including the works of Edelfelt, Schjerfbeck, and Halonen—and modern work by Picasso, Miro, and Henry Moore. It also boasts Finland's sole collection of pre-Columbian American Indian art and some fine Chinese Ming and Shang dynasty pieces.

FINLANDIA HOUSE

Mannerheimintie 9
00100 Helsinki
358 (0)9 402 41
finlandiahall@fin.hel.fi
Finlandia Hall was designed in 1962 and built between 1967 and 1972. The hall itself exhibits many of the ideas that Aalto experimented

with during his lifelong preoccupation with monumental building construction. The visitor can admire the preoccupation with detail and the high-quality work so typical of Aalto. Finlandia Hall is now the most famous venue in Helsinki for concerts, conferences, and exhibitions.

GALERIE ANHAVA

Mannerheiminaukis 3
00100 Helsinki
358 (0)9 66 99 89
www.anhava.com

GALERIE FORSBLOM

Pohjoisesplanandi 27C
00100 Helsinki

358 (0)9 680 3700
www.galerieforsblom.com
A newly renovated space for major art, Galerie Forsblom is well located in the heart of Helsinki city and specializes in modern and contemporary international and Finnish art.

GALLERIA SCULPTOR

Eteläranta 12
00130 Helsinki
358 (0)9 62 16337

HELSINKI CITY TENNISPALATSI ART MUSEUM

Salomonkatu 15
00100 Helsinki
358 (0)9 31087001

KAMPPI CENTER: A NEW URBAN FOCUS IN THE HEART OF HELSINKI

Helsinki's ever-changing silhouette is undergoing one of its biggest changes, as the new Kamppi Center emerges in the heart of the city. As the most expansive single construction project in the history of the Finnish capital, the resulting complex of underground bus and subway stations, apartment homes, market square, pedestrian space, and other urban facilities adds a fresh pulse to Helsinki. The Center occupies an open, windswept space that previously served as one of the city's main bus stations—and much further back, as an eighteenth-century military drill ground. Bus travelers will be grateful for the new subterranean shelter provided for their transport services.

A six-story shopping mall provides the focus above ground, with park and market squares expanding as aprons between the edifices. The steel and concrete load-bearing structure of the shopping center, with the long-distance bus terminals concealed below, presented special challenges to the office of architect Juhani Pallasmaa. The result is a welcoming hub of commerce, transport, and accommodation that sits well with the surrounding buildings, including the two "palaces": the Functionalist Glass Palace, built in 1936, and the Tennis Palace, which started life as vehicle service center in 1938 and has survived spells as a flea market and a sports hall.

www.kampinkeskus.fi/english

www.taidemuseo.fi
Part of a converted sports hall that is shared with a movie theater complex, a museum of culture, and various shops and restaurants, this branch of the Helsinki City Art Museum has staged highly successful changing shows, ranging from William Blake to Jeff Koons.

KIASMA: THE MUSEUM OF CONTEMPORARY ART
Mannerheiminaukio 2
00100 Helsinki
358 (0)9 1733 6501
www.kiasma.fi
This extraordinary building by American architect Steven Holl opened in 1998 to a mixed reception. Within a few years, however, it had gained almost affectionate acceptance as a Helsinki landmark. Housing the contemporary branch of the Finnish National Gallery, Kiasma does not exhibit its permanent collections but displays thematic shows focused on avant-garde artists, installations, and video projects. Many visitors are bemused by the exhibitions, but few emerge without having a reaction to express. Kiasma's café and well-stocked art bookshop are also very popular.

MANNERHEIM MUSEUM
Kalliolinnantie 14
00140 Helsinki
358 (0)9 635 443
www.mannerheim-museo.fi
This is the former home (rented from the founder of the modern confectionery company, Karl Fazer) of national hero and statesman, C.G.E. Mannerheim (1867–1951), whose horse-borne statue provides a monumental contrast to the

Kiasma Museum of Contemporary Art. The Mannerheim Museum is in the peaceful, scenic area of villas above the Kaivopuisto park. Mannerheim was a totemic figure in Finnish history. A soldier in the Russian imperial army until the 1917 revolution, he then went on to lead the eventually triumphant White Army against the Reds in the brutal Finnish Civil War in 1918. Later he took command of the Finnish armed forces in the Winter and Continuation Wars against Russia. After these wars, he served briefly as president.

MARITIME MUSEUM OF FINLAND
Hylkysaari
00570 Helsinki
358 (0)9 4050 9051
www.nba.fi/en/mmf
The lightship *Kemi* is a highlight of the **Maritime Museum of Finland**, on the small island (Hylkysaari) adjacent to the island of Korkeasaari, where Helsinki's zoo is located. It is reached by crossing a footbridge from Korkeasaari (bus 11 from Herttoniemi Metro, or on foot from Kulosaari). The museum charts Finland's maritime background, from coastal wrecks to the state-of-the-art, computerized icebreakers berthed across the harbor at Katajanokka.

MEILAHTI ART MUSEUM
Tamminiementie 6
00250 Helsinki
358 (0)9 310 87031
Reserved for changing exhibitions and another branch of the Helsinki City Art Museum, a visit to Meilahti can be combined with a stroll in the nearby Seurasaari Open Air Museum.

NATIONAL MUSEUM
www.nba.fi/en/nmfat
Mannerheimintie 34
00101 Helsinki
358 (0)9 4050 9544
kansallismuseo@nba.fi
Finland's National Museum is opposite the Finlandia Hall. It is the ultimate embodiment of the National Romantic style, borrowing Jugendstil, art nouveau, and rustic vernacular styles. A stone sculpture of a bear greets visitors at the top of the steps and the granite walls are decorated with fairy-tale relief. The resulting effect is that of a palace straight out of Tolkien. The building was the work of the Gesellius, Lindgren, and Saarinen team and was opened to the public in 1916. The exhibits housed here chart Finland's development from prehistory through agrarian peasantry to contemporary technological sophistication. Highlights include the czar's throne, occupied by the Russian ruler when Finland was a Grand Duchy from 1809 to 1917, and a painting called *The Attack* by Eetu Isto, which portrays the maid of Finland resisting the Russian eagle. The fresco in the entrance represents a mythical scene from Finland's national epic, *The Kalevala*, by Akseli Gallen-Kallela.

SEURASAARI
Seurasaari
00250 Helsinki
358 (0)9 4050 9660 in summer;
358 (0)9 4050 9574 in winter
seurasaavenulkomuseo@nba.fi
The Open-Air Museum of Seurasaari is a few miles to the north of the center (take the number 24 bus from the Swedish Theater), yet feels as if it could be right out in the middle of

the countryside. Traditional Finnish wooden dwellings and other buildings—including an entire manor, a church, and farm outhouses—have been brought here and reconstructed on a quiet, thickly wooded island which is approached by means of a long wooden causeway. The island is open throughout the year, although access to most of the buildings can only be gained in the summer for a fee of 4.50 euros (free for under 18s). Guides dressed in traditional costume explain the history of the buildings to visitors.

SINEBRYCHOFF ART MUSEUM
Bulevardi 40
00120 Helsinki
358 (0)9 1733 6460
www.sinebrychoffintaidemuseo.fi
As the third "arm" of the Finnish National Gallery, the Sinebrychoff Art Museum houses Old Masters, including European art—English, Spanish, Dutch, Flemish, Italian, and French—from the fourteenth century to the early nineteenth century, as well as a special collection of old Swedish portraits and miniatures.

SPORT MUSEUM OF FINLAND
Paavo Nurmentie 1
00250 Helsinki
358 (0)9 434 2250
urheilumuseo@stadion.fi
This museum is part of the Olympic Stadium and describes glorious landmarks in the history of Finnish sport. The Helsinki Olympics in 1952, for which the Stadium was built, is one of these, and the shoe—now gold-plated—worn by Paavo Nurmi on his gold medal run at the 1924 Paris Olympics takes

pride of place. Maverick ski jumper Matti Nykänen's medal collection is also on show, and the oldest exhibit is a 2,500-year-old ski. The museum also includes a sports library and an archive of a thousand sports posters. The Olympic Stadium Tower is another attraction nearby: take the lift to the top for excellent views across the city.

SUOMENLINNA

www.suomenlinna.fi
Built across a small archipelago at the entrance to the South Harbor and easily accessible by means of a twenty-minute ferry ride from the main Market Square, the island fortress of Suomenlinna is Helsinki's most exciting historical attraction. It is worth a visit at any time of the year and the ferries never stop running, even if the harbor is packed with thick ice in winter.
The fortress—the construction of which was begun under Swedish rule in 1748—is scattered across its own small archipelago, and its rocky shores and romantic ramparts are great places for summer picnics and brisk winter walks alike. The various small museums and, in summer, gallery shops, as well as an excellent visitor center, add cultural interest. Suomenlinna provides inspiration for visiting artists at the Nordic Institute for Contemporary Art guest studios. Cafés, restaurants, and a highly recommended macro-brewery bar serve refreshments. Suomenlinna's small permanent community includes the cadets at the Naval Academy, while its services consist of a shop and post office, library, and health center.
Visitor Center: tel. 09 684 1850/1880.

Doll and Toy Museum: tel. 09 668 417.
The Second World War **Vesikko submarine**: tel. 09 181 46238.
Coastal Artillery Museum: tel. 09 1814 5295/6.
Customs Museum: tel. 09 614 2394.

TAIDEHALLI (KUNSTHALLE)

Nervanderinkatu 3
00100 Helsinki
358 (0)9 454 2060
info@taidehalli.fi
The Kunsthalle, protected as a significant architectural monument, is a prominent example of 1920s neoclassicism in Finland. For more than seven decades, the Kunsthalle has been a leading Finnish venue for temporary exhibitions, with visual art from Finland and abroad, and developments in architecture, applied arts, and photography.

More museums in Helsinki:
Natural History Museum, covering Finnish flora and fauna, at Pohjoinen Rautatiekatu 13 (tel. 09 1912 8800).
The **Museum of Cultures** in the Tennispalatsi (tel. 09 40 501).
The **Finnish Museum of Photography** (tel. 09 6866 3621), the **Theater Museum** (tel. 09 6850 9150), and the **Hotel and Restaurant Museum** (tel. 09 6859 3700) are to be found at the **Cable Factory** arts and culture complex, Tallberginkatu 1G.
The **Post Museum** is at the main post office: entrance at Asema-aukio 5 (tel. 0204 514 908).
The **Museum of Finnish Architecture** at Kasarmikatu 24 (tel. 09 8567 5100).
The **Museum of Art and Design** at Korkeavuorenkatu 23 (tel. 09 622

0540) presents displays of Finnish design classics and some special exhibitions.

CHURCHES

TEMPPELIAUKIO CHURCH
Lutherinkatu 3 (end of Fredriksgatan)
00100 Helsinki
Dug into the rock, built at the end of the 1960s.

USPENSKI ORTHODOX CATHEDRAL
On the edge of the Katajanokka promontory stands Uspenski Cathedral, the biggest Orthodox Cathedral in Western Europe and another dominant feature on Helsinki's central skyline. Its evocative onion spires and red brick are in historical and architectural contrast to the nearby Lutheran Cathedral. It was built under Russian rule in 1868. The cathedral is a place of worship for the minority who practice the Orthodox faith in Finland. Uspenski is worth visiting just to admire the colorful icons, frescoes, and other decorations. From the terrace outside the main door visitors enjoy a fine view back over the Lutheran Cathedral and the Senate Square, the President's Palace and the Market Square.

ATTRACTIONS

LASIPALATSI FILM AND MEDIA CENTER
Mannerheimintie 22-24
00100 Helsinki
Opposite the Kiasma, the building dates to the 1930s (see the Ravintola Latipalatsi). Renovated

during the late 1990s for multi-media activities, it has retained its original 1930s neon signs.

SENATE SQUARE
The gleaming white splendor of the **Lutheran Cathedral** is Helsinki's classic landmark. Like most of the buildings around the spacious Senate Square, it was designed by German architect C.L. Engel (1778–1840). Engel was commissioned to supervise the new Empire-style center when Helsinki took over the role of capital from Turku when Finland became a Grand Duchy of the Russian Empire in 1809. The cathedral was consecrated in 1852. The **Bank of Finland**, the **House of Estates**, the **National Archives**, the **House of Nobility**, and the **University Library** complete the harmonious and dignified entity in and around the Senate Square, which is dominated by a statue of Tsar Alexander II. Helsinki City Hall is on the Market Square side of the so-called Lion Quarter, while much of **Helsinki University** is also close by. The intimate **Orthodox Church of the Holy Trinity** is in Unioninkatu, near to the Lutheran Cathedral.
The little cobbled streets leading down to the Market Square and lined with some small shops and cafés include the museum street of Sokfiankatu, which traces the history of urban evolution from the 1850s to the 1930s. **Café Engel**, a cozy favorite, is opposite the cathedral. Helsinki's oldest building (from 1757), the former home of merchant Johan Sederholm, is on one corner of the square, at Aleksanterinkatu 16-18, and is open to the public as a museum (tel. 09 169 3625).

THE FINNISH CALENDAR

Firework displays are a popular way of welcoming the **New Year** at midnight on **DECEMBER 31**. The show can be quite spectacular if you find yourself a vantage point with a view across the city.

• **JANUARY 6:** is **Epiphany**, or Twelfth Night, and a public holiday in Finland. The days grow gradually longer in January, although in parts of Lapland in the far north the sun barely peeps above the horizon. Spring comes late to Finland, and snow covers the whole country through February and March. Various events and festivals punctuate the winter months. In late January, older schoolchildren celebrate the imminent end of classes in a city center parade.

• **FEBRUARY 5:** is **J.L. Runeberg Day**, in honor of the nineteenth-century national poet and composer of the words to the national anthem. The Finnish flag is flown on this and other designated flag days. Laskiainen marks the start of Lent, and is the time for sledging outings. Anywhere in the city with a slope serves the purpose: in Helsinki, the Observatory hill in the Kaivopuisto park is one of the most popular, and the Paloheinä ski slope in the Central Park is another.

• **FEBRUARY 28: Kalevala Day** is a celebration of the national epic of the same name.

• On **Palm Sunday**, you may find yourself surrounded by groups of girls carrying willow branches and reciting charms: they are acting out a version of the Orthodox *virpominen* tradition, and the willow switch is meant to bring good luck. The girls will expect sweets or money in return.

• The **Easter** holiday is quiet, and Helsinki can be particularly sleepy at this time. The emphasis is on religious celebration and family gatherings.

• **MAY 1: Vappu**, and the night preceding it, brings the liveliest celebration of the year, since it marks the beginning of spring. The streets in the towns become the scenes of wild outdoor parties, and this is the traditional time for people to don their white student matriculation hats—a tradition that has echoes in other parts of the Nordic region. There is an understandable sense of relief in the air as the last vestiges of winter are left behind and the long days of summer lie ahead.

• There is a saying that if one lacks a lover at *helluntai*, **Whitsun**, then one will not have a lover for the coming summer. *Helatorstai* (**Ascension Day**) is a public holiday.

• **JUNE 12: Helsinki Day**, the official anniversary of the city's foundation is marked with all sorts of events. The **Midsummer** weekend is the one closest to the longest day of the year, and many Finns depart from the cities to spend this weekend at the thousands of cabins and holiday homes all over Finland. The Seurasaari Open Air Museum is the setting for lively traditional celebrations, including bonfires, a traditional wedding, and dancing.

• An air of magic dominates in summer, when the light extends to midnight in the south and well into the early hours in the far north. Nobody would guarantee sustained beautiful weather in Finland in the summer, but the chances of warm and languid days are good.

Crayfish parties in August, based on a Swedish tradition, provide a final opportunity to savor the summer evenings before the trees erupt in a glorious display of autumnal color. In Lapland, this display—known as *ruska*—merits a special trip. At the beginning of October, dancing and accordion music fills the Market Square in Helsinki as the traditional **Herring Fair** draws fishermen and farmers from the archipelago to sell their wares.

• On **All Saints Day**, candles placed on the graves of deceased loved ones illuminate cemeteries up and down the country: it is a touching spectacle.

• **DECEMBER 6: Independence Day** commemorates Finland's hard-won departure from Russian rule in 1917. According to tradition, two candles are placed in windows at six in the evening. A procession of dignitaries and celebrities files through the President's Palace in Helsinki at the Independence Day Ball, while a torch-lit procession moves from the grave of Marshall Mannerheim in Hietaniemi to the Senate Square.

• By now, thoughts are turning to **Christmas**. The main streets in central Helsinki are decorated with lights, and the Tuomas Christmas market opens in the Esplanade park. "Little Christmas" parties—*pikkujoulut*—are held by companies for their staff in advance of Christmas proper, when families gather for cozy celebrations at home.

SOUTHERN FINLAND

HOTELS

HOTEL-RESTAURANT FISKARS-WÄRDSHUS
Wärdshus 1836
10470 Fiskars
358 (0)19 276 6510
www.fiskarsvillage.net
warssy@wardshus.inet.fi
This hotel boasts a good restaurant and fine design, as well as modern rooms.

MUSTIO MANOR
Hållsnäsintie 89
10360 Mustio
358 (0)19 36 231
myyntipalvelu@mustionlinna.fi
The Merlin Tower and Orangerie suites at one of Finland's best-preserved manor estates are the pick of the accommodation at Mustio. The peaceful, picturesque parkland provides the perfect retreat for explorers of southern Finland and is pitched halfway between the cities of Turku and Helsinki. Tastefully restrained rooms with all facilities, and a fine restaurant in converted stables.

NAANTALI SPA AND SUNBORN YACHT HOTEL
Matkailijantie 2
21100 Naantali
358 (0)2 44 550
For a therapeutic break in relaxing surroundings, the Naantali Spa is hard to beat. The small old town of Naantali, with its wonderful wooden villas and popular summer yachting marina, is a stroll away; the awe-inspiring archipelago is on the horizon. The hotel will spoil you with its spa treatments, and the Sunborn

Princess yacht berthed nearby adds an extra dimension of luxury with its 140 sea-facing suites.

GRÄNNÄS BED & BREAKFAST
21660 Nagu
358 (0)2 4651188
Grännäs in Nagu (Swedish name for Nauvo), in the middle of the beautiful Turku archipelago, is located in a converted former cavalry estate dating to the middle of the eighteenth century and is hosted by Lisbet and Hans Granqvist. Guests stay in the recently renovated "bailiff's residence" containing five individual double rooms, a spacious breakfast room, and a small TV room. The house is surrounded by a garden in which guests can enjoy their breakfast or prepare a barbecue dinner.

HAIKKO MANOR
Haikkoontie 114
06400 Porvoo
358 (0)19 576 01
A fabulous mansion on a slope overlooking spacious, leafy grounds leading down to the water, the present Haikko manor dates from 1914, but there have been manors here since the fifteenth century. The quaint old town of Porvoo is nearby, and Helsinki is an hour's drive away. Hints of the elegant Gustavian style adorn the interior. The hotel also runs a separate spa and fitness center.

BENGTSKÄR LIGHTHOUSE
25950 Rosala
358 (0)2 4667227
info@bengtskär.fi

Open from May to September, this remote lighthouse off the southern Finnish archipelago is the ultimate bed and breakfast getaway. The lighthouse stands on a rugged skerry with open sea in every direction and offers simple but comfortable and—when the wind is howling outside—extremely cozy accommodation.

PARK HOTEL
Rauhankatu 1
20100 Turku
358 (0)2 2732 555
An independent, quiet oasis right in the heart of the city of Turku and close to the railway station, the Park Hotel is a riot of art nouveau chic. Built in 1902, it has retained every ounce of its original character, with quirky antiques in each of the unique rooms. The friendliness of its staff—including the trademark resident parrot in reception—ensures that your stay will be memorable.

SOKOS HOTEL HAMBURGER BÖRS
Kauppiaskatu 6
Turku
358 (0)2 337 381
The very central location makes this one of Turku's favorite hotels for both business and leisure visitors. The bustling market square is on the doorstep, and the beautiful riverside historical center is a short walk away. The hotel's 346 rooms are fitted in typically Nordic clean and efficient style, and guests have a swimming pool, three saunas, and seven restaurants at their disposal.

RESTAURANTS AND CAFÉS

RESTAURANT RUSELL
Eckerövägen 446
22270 Eckerö
358 (0)18 38499
restaurang.rusell@aland.net
Housed in a beautiful wooden sailing pavilion, Rusell offers a leisurely haven close to the village of Eckerö and its increasingly popular golf course. The menu comprises typical archipelago specialties, including shellfish soup, perch, and deer, as well as desserts made from the vitamin-C-rich sea buckthorn berry.

INDIGO RESTAURANT AND BAR
Nygatan 1
22100 Mariehamn
358 (0)18 16550
indigo@aland.net
Indigo is in a red-brick house in the center of the capital of the Swedish-speaking Åland archipelago, and the location gives a homely old-world feel to the place. There is nothing old world about the menu, however, which embraces cosmopolitan influences from far and wide. The bar also offers a separate bistro menu.

RESTAURANT NAUTICAL
Hamngatan 2
22100 Mariehamn
358 (0)18 19931
restaurang@nautical.inet.fi
Tasteful blue furniture and fittings echo the seafaring theme at Nautical, the windows of which look out on the superb museum ship, the four-mast Åland bark *Pommern*, and the

harbor of Mariehamn. Archipelago fish figure high on the menu, although duck, lamb, and deer are also on offer, along with a global wine list.

CAFÉ AMANDIS
Nunnakatu 5
21100 Naantali
358 (0)2 430 8774
By the waterfront, a nice wooden place dating to 1900 that offers homemade cakes.

RESTAURANT MERISALI
Nunnakatu 1
21100 Naantali
358 (0)2 435 2451
Merisali is by the harbor and close to the beautiful church, a venue for an annual music festival, in the easygoing seaside town of Naantali. The archipelago buffet, with selections of salted and pickled fish, roes, rich dark breads, and salads, is the specialty here. After their meal, diners can relax on the outdoor terrace, watch the yachts come and go, and listen to live music wafting across the water.

RESTAURANT L'ESCALE
Strandvägen 1
21660 Nauvo (Nagu)
358 (0)2 4604400
This archipelago surprise takes an hour to reach by boat or road from Turku, but diners are rewarded with a quayside restaurant that mixes French flair with regional flavors and ingredients. Perch and salmon head the fish dish selection, but they are just samples of an extensive and very reasonably priced choice. A boathouse grill

serves up archipelago banquets. There is an extremely impressive wine list, dominated by French wines, and guests can sample one of the six varieties of snaps made in the adjacent distillery by restaurateur Mikael Smeds. Well worth making the detour.

WANHA LAAMANNI
Vuorikatu 17
06100 Porvoo
358 (0)19 523 0455
wanha.laamanni@wanhalaamanni.fi
Wanha Laamanni is in the center of Porvoo's uniquely picturesque old wooden town, an hour's drive to the east of Helsinki, in an eighteenth-century house close to the cathedral. A welcoming open fireplace greets diners on the top floor, while the menu embraces duck, lamb, perch, and reindeer.

HERMANNI
Läntinen Rantakatu
20100 Turku
A comfortable brasserie-style venue with good food by the river.

RAVINTOLA SAMPPALINNA
Itäinen Rantakatu 10
10 700 Turku
358 (0)9 251 1000
In the summer do not miss this restaurant in a lacy wooden villa overlooking the Aura river. Great for a smörgåsbord lunch of assorted herrings, salmon, cold cuts with new potatoes, and salads.

ROCCA
Läntinen Rantakatu, 55
20100 Turku
This restaurant has people coming

from out of town. Excellent food and trendy elegant atmosphere.

MUSEUMS

TARVASPÄÄ
The Gallen-Kallela Museum
Gallen-Kallelan tie 27
02600 Espoo
358 (0)9 541 3388
www.gallen-kallela.fi
Finland's national artist, Akseli Gallen-Kallela, designed and built this studio home here, just to the west of Helsinki, in 1911–1913. In 1961 Tarvaspää opened to the public as the Gallen-Kallela Museum. The Gallen-Kallela Museum collections reflect the versatility of the man, including paintings, drawings, graphics, sculpture, posters, photographs, and works of applied art, as well as personal items and documents. The house, located close to the seashore, is half church, half castle, dominated by a fort-like tower.

HVITTRÄSK
Hvitträskintie 166
02440 Luoma
358 (0)9 4 050 9630
www.nba.fi/en/hvittrask
hvittrask@nba.fi
To the west of the capital, shielded by trees at the top of a steep slope overlooking a lake of the same name, is Hvitträsk, the former studio home of architects Herman Gesellius, Armas Lindgren, and Eliel Saarinen. This enchanting indulgence in National Romantic and Finnish art nouveau is one of the most rewarding destinations for short excursions from the capital. Visitors can follow the

steep steps down to the lakeside sauna (advance reservations can be made through the restaurant), or take another path to Saarinen's quiet forest grave.

MUSEUM SHIP POMMERN
22101 Mariehamn
Åland
358 (0)18 53142
pommern@mariehamn.aland.fi
The majestic four-mast bark, the *Pommern*, commissioned in 1903, is one of the landmarks of the West Harbor in Mariehamn, capital of the Åland archipelago province, and is a reminder of the fleet of sailing cargo ships that were once based in these islands. The excellent condition of the *Pommern* is unique, all other existing ships in her class having been rebuilt at some time. The museum ship co-operates with the nearby Åland Maritime Museum.

PORI ART MUSEUM
Eteläranta
28100 Pori
358 (0)2 621 1080
taidemuseo@pori.fi
Pori's Art Museum was founded by arts patron Maire Gullichsen and includes the collection of the foundation that bears her name, along with the Pori Municipal Collection. It is one of the most adventurous provincial art museums in Finland, housed by the river Kokemäki in a handsome former warehouse built in the nineteenth century.

SOUTHERN FINLAND

ABOA VETUS & ARS NOVA MUSEUMS
Itäinen Rantakatu 4-6
20700 Turku
358 (0)2 2500 552
info@aboavetusarsnova.fi
www.aboavetusarsnova.fi
Aboa Vetus, a museum of archeology and history, was built around an excavated medieval city block and took shape when a part of the old city of Turku —the second biggest city in Sweden when Finland was under that country's rule—was uncovered during renovation work on the Rettig Palace. The forgotten arched cellars and cobbled streets had lain buried underground for centuries. Aboa Vetus is adjacent to the Ars Nova Museum of Contemporary Art.

ARS NOVA MUSEUM
Itäinen Rantakatu 4-6
20700 Turku
358 (0)2 2500 552
info@aboavetusarsnova.fi
Turku's Museum of Contemporary Art is adjacent to its local history and archeology museum, Aboa Vetus, close to the Aura river, and the venue for the Turku Biennale.

PHARMACY MUSEUM AND QWENSEL HOUSE
Läntinen Rantakatu 13
20101 Turku
358 (0)2 262 0280
The Qwensel House is Turku's oldest bourgeois residence. The rococo and Gustavian rooms evoke something of the lifestyle of the ruling classes during the period of Swedish rule in Finland. The Qwensel House also houses

the Pharmacy Museum, a fascinating collection of pharmaceutical instruments and paraphernalia from various sources.

TURKU ART MUSEUM
Aurakatu 26
20100 Turku
358 (0)2 2627 100
www.turuntaidemuseo.fi
The modernized Turku Art Museum reopened its doors in April 2005, offering its audience the Finnish history of art from the early days to the latest contemporary media art. International works of art and Scandinavian art in particular dominate the exhibits, housed in a magnificent National Romantic granite building above the city center.

WÄINÖ AALTONEN MUSEUM OF ART
Itäinen Rantakatu 38
20810 Turku
358 (0)2 2620 850
The Wäinö Aaltonen Museum Collection, part of the Turku City Art Museum, contains works of art purchased by or donated to the City of Turku since 1937. The most significant aspects of the collection are the sculptures, paintings, graphics, and drawings by the sculptor Wäinö Aaltonen, fellow of the Finnish Academy of Arts.

THE LAKES

HOTELS

IMATRA VALTIONHOTELLI (State Hotel)
Torkkelinkatu 2
55100 Imatra
358 (0)15 688 81
This glorious fortress of a hotel, with its turrets and balconies, is a celebration of the National Romantic style and dates from 1903 when Finland was still a Grand Duchy of the Russian Empire. The border with Russia is a short drive away, and the famous rapids on the Vuoksi river are just behind the hotel.

HOTEL KOLI
Ylä-Kolintie 39
83960 Koli
358 (0)13 6887 100
Magnificent views across Lake Pielinen—probably the best lake views in Finland—greet guests in most of the rooms of this hotel perched atop the Ukko-Koli ridge in Finnish Karelia. The classic sprawling scenery here is celebrated in the art of various Finnish artists, including Eero Järnefelt and Pekka Halonen. Guests can be carried from the car park by a special trolley car up to the hotel.

HOTEL ISOVALKEINEN
Päiväranta
70420 Kuopio
358 (0)17 5396 100
Hotel IsoValkeinen, a modern but welcoming lakeside hotel, is just over three miles (5 km) from the center of Kuopio, a pleasant hub for summer lakeland steamer traffic and a popular venue for spectacular ski-jumping events in winter. The hotel is proud of its sauna complex, right at the water's edge, complete with outdoor hot tub.

KEKKOLAN KARTANO OY
Vanharmäentie 36
50600 Mikkeli
358 (0)15 230 474
kekkola@kekkolankartano.fi
Restaurant, bed & breakfast—a good place.

PUNKAHARJUN VALTIONHOTELLI (Punkaharju State Hotel)
58450 Punkaharju
358 (0)15 739611
punkaharju.myynti@lomaliitto.fi
This beautiful and romantic wooden villa dating from 1845 nestles at the foot of the Punkaharju ridge and is a handy base for Savonlinna (twelve miles (20 km) away) and its annual opera festival, the Forest Museum at Lusto, and the Retretti Arts Center. The twenty-four rooms are situated in the main building and in the nearby Empress's Villa.

SPA HOTEL CASINO
Kasinonsaari Pb 60
57101 Savonlinna
358 (0)15 73950
A lakeside retreat on its own island close to the center of this city that springs into life during the annual Opera Festival held in the impressive castle. The Spa Hotel Casino is one of the most hotly sought-after hotels for visiting opera buffs from all over the world, and is a quiet and comfortable base for Lakeland explorations at other times.

SCANDIC HOTEL ROSENDAHL
Pyynikintie 13
33230 Tampere
358 (0)3 244 1111
Blessed with 213 spacious and elegant rooms, the large size of this modern hotel against the soaring backdrop of the beautiful pine-covered

ridge of Pyynikki is offset by the scale of the broad Pyhäjärvi lake, on the banks of which it is situated. The city center of Tampere is easily accessible.

SOKOS HOTEL TAMMER
Satakunnankatu 13
33230 Tampere
358 (0)3 262 6265
Retaining its original 1920s charm and originally known as the Grand Hotel Tammer, this is one of Tampere's most desirable places to stay. The attractive red brick is in keeping with the converted mill buildings near the rapids that run through the center of Tampere. Tall arches and chandeliers grace the excellent restaurant.

RESTAURANTS

MUSTA LAMMAS
Satamakatu 4
70100 Kuopio
358 (0)17 5810 458
ravintola@mustalammas.net
In the atmospheric cellar of a former brewery built in the 1860s, Musta Lammas ("black sheep") is part of the *Chaine de Rotisseurs*—rare outside Helsinki—close to the lake steamer port of Kuopio. It serves a delightful menu that makes the most of local fish, lamb, and beef, as well as vegetarian options.

FINLAYSONIN PALATSI
Kuninkaankatu 1
33210 Tampere
358 (0)3 260 5770
Finlaysonin Palatsi means "Finlayson's Palace" and is named after the textile mill industrialist whose company was founded and thrived in Tampere. This splendid

manor is near the rapids that run through the city and is a gloriously preserved treasury of nineteenth-century industrial affluence. The menu combines continental ideas with fresh Finnish flavors. A great wine list, too. The summer terrace provides relaxation from the nearby city center.

HELLA & HUONE
Salhojankatu 48
500 Tampere
358 (0)3 253 2440
hella@huone.info
A romantic cozy hideaway with just thirty-three seats close to Tampere's Tampere Hall venue, Hella & Huone prides itself on a French menu, including a Menu Gourmand starting with *petit pain de foie gras*, progressing through *paupiette de veau* and rounded off with *assiette de chocolat*. One of Finland's best authentic French restaurants.

LATERNA
Puutarhakatu 11
Tampere
358 (0)3 272 0241
aleksi@aleksinravintolat.fi
The Laterna is one of Tampere's oldest restaurants and recent renovations have sacrificed none of the Slavic atmosphere enhanced by the antique furniture, objects, and paintings. Blinis and palmeni are among the items on a menu that has a distinctively Russian flavor.

MUSEUMS

ART CENTER SALMELA
Mäntyharjuntie 25
52700 Mäntyharju
358 (0)15 464 526

www.taidekeskussalmela.fi
A privately-owned summer gallery in traditional Karelian style in a peaceful parkland setting, Salmela is a welcome attraction at Mäntyharju on the edge of Finland's eastern lakeland. As well as championing the cause of Finnish artists and sculptors, Salmela also arranges concerts in the church at Mäntyharju which have consistently attracted top class performers, such as the Helsinki Philharmonic Orchestra.

RETRETTI ART CENTER
58450 Punkaharju
358 (0)15 775 22 00
www.retretti.fi
In the heart of Finnish lakeland and close to the picturesque Punkaharju ridge, Retretti has galleries both above and below ground. The subterranean cave galleries and concert hall (a supplementary venue for performances of the Opera Festival at nearby Savonlinna), quarried in the 1980s to a depth of ninety-eight feet (30 m), provide a unique and atmospheric exhibition space covering forty thousand square feet (3,700 sq. m). The excellent annual exhibitions make the most of this extraordinary setting.

LENIN MUSEUM
Hämeenpuisto 28
33200 Tampere
358 (0)3 276 8100
lenin@sci.fi
The only permanent Lenin Museum in the world is at the Worker's Hall in Tampere, in the hall where Lenin and Stalin met for the first time in 1905. The museum collects, exhibits, and researches material

dealing with Lenin's life and the history of the Soviet Union/Russia, especially where this is related to Finland and the Finns.

SARA HILDÉN ART MUSEUM
Särkänniemi
33230 Tampere
358 (0)3 3144 3500
sara.hilden@tampere.fi
The Sara Hildén Art Museum is far more important than the Tampere Museum of Contemporary Art and can be called Finland's foremost collection of modern and contemporary art. It is the permanent home of the collection of modern Finnish and international art owned by the Sara Hildén Foundation and maintained by the City of Tampere. The collection numbers some 3,300 works presenting a cross section of the development in modern art over the last forty years.

TAMPERE MUSEUM OF CONTEMPORARY ART
Museum Center Vapriikki
Veturiaukio 4
33101 Tampere
358 (0)3 31466966
vapriikki@tampere.fi
Part of the Museum Center Vapriikki in ingeniously converted industrial buildings in the center of Tampere, this museum stages inspired changing exhibitions and includes an absorbing archive of black and white photographs.

NORTHERN FINLAND (LAPLAND)

HOTELS

LAPLAND HOTEL KILPIS
99490 Kilpisjärvi
358 (0)16 537 761
kilpis@laplandhotels.com
Situated at the very northwestern tip of Finnish Lapland, close to the borders with Norway and Sweden, the Hotel Kilpis is a favorite oasis for fell trekkers. One of Finland's few real mountains, Saana, looms on one side, while the broad expanse of the Kilpis lake extends on the other.

LEVI CENTER HULLU PORO
99 130 Levi
358 (0)916 651 0100
hullu.poro@levi.fi
The only Finnish ski resort to host a Alpine skiing World Cup event, Levi is the center of an active legendary night life at the Hullu Poro, a hotel and restaurant complex featuring concerts and great Lapp food served in a memorable traditional Kota surrounding.

LAPLAND HOTEL PALLAS
99330 Pallastunturi
358 (0)16 532 441
The Pallastunturi fell attracts skiers in winter and fell trekkers in summer and during the colorful natural explosion of fall. The Hotel Pallas nestles in the fells in a gloriously remote and otherwise scenically desolate spot. Like all Lapland hotels, the hotel boasts warm rooms, a fine restaurant, and a soothing sauna.

LAPLAND HOTEL SKY OUNASVAARA
96400 Rovaniemi
358 (0)16 335 3311
The Sky Hotel is on the top of the Ounasvaara fell just over a mile from the center of Rovaniemi, the provincial capital of Finnish Lapland. Forty-seven of the fifty-eight rooms have their own saunas and the restaurant looks out across the classic Lapp fell landscape. Ski trails lead into the forest, and the rooftop is a favorite spot for Japanese tourists admiring the Northern Lights.

RESTAURANTS

FOREST MANOR
Joulumaantie 1
96930 Arctic Circle
358 (0)1 369 056
ounasvaaran.pirtit@co.inet.fi
A charming old forest owner's manor converted into a private restaurant, just outside the Lapp city of Rovaniemi. It includes a *kota*, or Lapp teepee, with its own fish and reindeer menu.

HIRSIPIRTTI RESTAURANT
97610 Oikarainen
358 (0)40 706 7680
About twelve miles (20 km) from Rovaniemi, on the banks of the Kymijoki river, Hirsipirtti is located in a handsome log cabin and serves Lapp specialties.

RESTAURANT HEHKU AT HOTEL SIRKANTÄHTI
99130 Sirkka
358 (0)16 640 100
sirkantahti@laplandhotels.com
The Taste of the North menu at this Lapland restaurant uses only fresh local ingredients from the north of Finland, Sweden, and Norway. This means treats such as reindeer soup, glow-fried salmon, and desserts made from Lapland berries, as well as various other fish and reindeer dishes. Located in the center of the Levi ski resort.

MUSEUMS

SIIDA: SÁMI MUSEUM AND NORTHERN LAPLAND NATURE CENTER
Inarintie
99870 Inari
358 (0)16 665 212
siida@samimuseum.fi
www.samimuseum.fi/english
SIIDA is the home of the Sámi Museum and the Northern Lapland Nature Center in Inari in the far north of Finland. Hosting cultural and nature exhibitions, and housed in a building that was designed in partnership between Juhani Pallasmaa and Tapio Wirkkala (but completed after the death of Wirkkala), it is a meeting place and an exhibition center that provides visitors with new information about Sámi, or Lapp, culture and the natural environment of Northern Lapland.

SNOW CASTLE
Torikatu 2
94100 Kemi
358 (0)16 259 502
info@snowcastle.net
www.snowcastle.net
With a decade of snow architecture behind it, the Snow Castle by the harbor in Kemi on the northern shore of the Gulf of Bothnia is a wondrous creation and includes a Snow Hotel, a bar, restaurant, art galleries, a sauna, concert performances, and a truly spooky chapel. The features vary in style from year to year, and the Castle usually lasts from its New Year opening date until around the beginning of April when it melts!

ARKTIKUM
Pohjoisranta 4
96100 Rovaniemi
358 (0)16 341 2
www.arktikum.fi
Housing the Provincial Museum of Lapland and an Arctic Center, opened in 1992 and designed by the Danish team of Bonderup-Thorup-Waade, Arktikum is a unique arcade that radiates from a central glass-roofed axis that extends like a glistening alien chrysalis down to the banks of the river running through the provincial capital, Rovaniemi. It houses excellent exhibits on Lapp (Sámi) culture and history and Arctic phenomena such as the Northern Lights or Aurora Borealis.

MORE USEFUL INTERNET LINKS

www.visitfinland.com
The portal for websites of the Finnish Tourist Board
www.hel.fi
Excellent portal to all Helsinki information
www.fmi.fi/en/index.html
Weather forecasts
http://virtual.finland.fi
Ministry for Foreign Affairs information pages in English
www.helsinkicard.com
Introduction to Helsinki Card
www.yle.fi/news
Finnish Broadcasting Company news
www.helsinki-hs.net
International version of the Helsinki daily paper
www.blue1.com
SAS subsidiary operating domestic flights in Finland (previously Air Botnia)
www.helsinkithisweek.net
Helsinki events and listings, restaurant information
www.sauna.fi
Culture and history of and information about sauna bathing tradition
www.vr.fi
Finnish State Railways: timetables, information
www.eckeroline.fi
Baltic ferry traffic
www.silja.fi
Silja Line, Baltic traffic
www.vikingline.fi
Viking Line, Baltic traffic
www.lindaline.fi
Hydrofoils to Tallinn
www.tallink.fi
Baltic traffic to Tallinn
www.njl.fi
Nordic Jet Line, traffic to Tallinn
www.expressbus.fi
Long distance coach travel

www.finnair.com
Finnish national airline
www.ilmailulaitos.fi
Helsinki airport flight information
www.pohjolanliikenne.fi
Long distance coach travel
www.matkahuolto.fi
Long distance coach travel
www.ytv.fi
Portal for Helsinki district public transport
www.finnexpo.fi
Details of exhibitions, events at Helsinki Fair Center
www.museoliitto.fi
Finnish Museums Association
www.nba.fi
National Board of Antiquities
www.laplandhotels.com
Major hotel chain in northern Finland
www.helsinkiexpert.fi
On-line tour shop and information; hotel booking
www.lomarengas.fi
Agency for holiday cabin accommodation
www.radissonsas.com
Hotel chain website
www.royalravintolat.com
Restaurant chain
www.scandic-hotels.com
Hotel chain website
www.sokoshotels.fi
Hotel chain website
www.lippupalvelu.fi
Ticket bookings
www.lippupiste.fi
Ticket bookings
www.tiketti.fi
Ticket bookings
www.stockmann.fi
Department store with branches in Helsinki, Tampere, and Turku
www.globalrefund.com
Tax-free shopping scheme site

BUYER'S GUIDE

UNITED STATES

FINNSTYLE
115 Washington Avenue North
Minneapolis, MN 55401-1619
United States
Tel.: +1 (612) 341-4075
info@finnstyle.com
www.finnstyle.com

FINNWARE
1116 Commercial Street
Astoria, OR 97103
United States
Tel.: +1 (800) 851-FINN (3466)
Fax: +1 (503) 325-0241
Email: finns@willapabay.org
Finnish, Swedish, Norwegian, Danish, and Icelandic products and handcrafted items made by Scandinavian artists of the lower Columbia River region.

INGEBRETSEN'S SCANDINAVIAN GIFTS & FOODS
1601 E. Lake Street
Minneapolis, MN 55407
United States
Tel.: +1 (612) 729-9333
Fax: +1 (612) 729-1243
Email: info@ingebretsens.com

THE KANTELE SHOP
1541 Clover Valley Road
Duluth, MN 55804
United States
Tel.: +1 (218) 525-7609
Email: gerry@kantele.com
Traditional Finnish musical instruments made by Gerry Henkel.

KIITOS MARIMEKKO
1262 Third Avenue
Between 72nd and 73rd Streets
New York, NY 10021
United States
Tel.: +1 (212) 628-8400
Fax +1 (212) 628-2814
Email: info@kiitosmarimekko.com
www.kiitosmarimekko.com
New York City boutique and online retailer of Marimekko apparel, housewares, accessories, handbags, shoes, as well as home decorating products and textiles.

MARIMEKKO NORTH AMERICA
111 South Broadway
Rochester, MN 55904
United States
Tel.: +1 (507) 261-6541
Email: info@marimekko.us
www.marimekko.us

MEMORIES OF FINLAND
Historic Savage Mill
8600 Foundry Street, Box 2043
Savage, MD 20763
United States
Tel.: +1 (800) 529-FINN (3466)
Fax: +1 (410) 828-1660
Finnish crafts and gifts.

NORTHERN LIGHTS
826 Santa Cruz Avenue
Menlo Park, CA 94025
United States
Tel.: +1 (650) 325-0313
Arts, crafts, books, and collectibles.

SCAN TRENDS
900 North Point Street
Ghirardelli Square
San Francisco, CA 94109
United States
Tel.: +1 (415) 775.2217
Scandinavian gifts.

THE WOODEN SPOON
1617 Avenue K
Plano, TX 75074
United States
Tel.: +1 (972) 424-6867
Email: twonordic@aol.com
Scandinavian gifts, food, and classes.

UNITED KINGDOM

MARIMEKKO
16/17 St. Christopher's Place
London, W1U 1NZ
United Kingdom
Tel.: +44 (0) 20 7486 6454
Fax: +44 (0) 20 7486 6456
Email: info@marimekko.co.uk
www.marimekko.co.uk
Apparel, housewares, accessories, handbags, shoes, as well as home decorating products and textiles.

BIBLIOGRAPY

Bird, Tim. *Hands-On Guide to Helsinki*. Helsinki: Tammi Publishing, 2004.
ISBN 9513129357

Harding, Paul. *Lonely Planet Guide to Finland*. Lonely Planet, 2003.
ISBN 1740590767

Jakobson, Max. *Finland in the New Europe*. Westport, CT.: Praeger, 1998.
ISBN 0275963713

Jussila, Osmo; Hentilä, Seppo; and Nevakivi, Jukka. *From Grand Duchy to a Modern State: A Political History of Finland since 1809*. London: Hurst, 1999.
ISBN 1850654212

Jutikkala, Eino and Pirinen Kauko. *A History of Finland*. Porvoo: WSOY, 2003.
ISBN 9510279110

Klinge, Matti. *Finland in Europe*. Helsinki: Otava, 2003.
ISBN 9511185667

Pesonen, Pertti. "Politics in Finland" in *Comparative Governance* by W. Phillips Shively. New York: McGraw-Hill, 2004.
ISBN 0256601534

Tillotson, H. M. *Finland at Peace & War*. Norwich: Michael Russel Publishing Ltd., 1996.
ISBN 0859552223

INDEX

INDEX

ACKNOWLEDGMENTS

Thanks to: Ingalill Snitt; Anna Hall and the Alvar Aalto Foundation; Professor Juhani Pallasmaa; Kirsten Ilander; Marjo Brunow-Ruola and Pekka Ruola; Per and Paula Wilson; Francis and Aila Weaver; Jukka Sirén; Panu Kaila; Arto Uunila; Tauno and Liisa Tarna; Rafaela Seppälä; Mika Hammarén (VirtualFinland); Christina von Haartman; Ritva Puotila; Eero Aarnio; Vuokko Nurmesniemi; Kati Heikkilä; Kari Virtanen; Tuomas Hoikkala; Anna Molander-Bry and the Finnish Tourist Board in Paris; my parents; and last but not least, my dear and supportive wife, Eeva-Helena Laurinsalo.

– Tim Bird

Thank you to everyone who kindly opened their door to me: Daniel Rozensztroch; Rafaela Seppälä; Tuomas Hoikkala; Elisabeth Nordin; Björn Linell; Marianne Eriksson; Seppo Jarva; Juhani Lemmetti; Gill Renlund; Karin Makowski; Marjatta Hapio; Ristomatti Ratia; Kaj Forsblom; Seppo Toivonen; Anna Molander; the Office du Tourisme in Paris; Gunnilla de la Chapelle; Tom Sarpaneva; Antti Siltavuori; Juhani Pallasmaa; and Ritva Puotila; as well as those who contributed to this project but cannot be included here due to space constraints.

– Ingalill Snitt

The publisher thanks Seppo Toivonen for his enthusiastic reception from the beginning of this project, as well as all of the individuals without whose support this book would never have been possible: Juhani Pallasmaa, who agreed to contribute the foreword, Suzanna de Bokay-Flammarion who conceived the subject and who followed it through to its publication, Christine Hägerström and Rafaela Seppälä for their hospitality in Finland, and Tuula Wyssmann and Anna Molander-Bry who provided a precious link between Paris and Finland. Finally, a sincere thank you to Isabelle Ducat who, by her talent and her unfailing eye, made it possible to publish this book in four simultaneous editions: English, French, Swedish, and Finnish. Thanks as well to the foreign editors who joined us in this endeavor.

Copyediting: Susan Schneider
Typesetting: Barbara Kekus
Proofreading: Ellen Booker
Color Separation: Reproscan
Maps: Édigraphie

Distributed in North America by Rizzoli International Publications.

Simultaneously published in French as
L'Art de Vivre en Finlande
© Flammarion, 2005

English-language edition
© Flammarion, 2005

87, quai Panhard et Levassor
75647 Paris cedex 13

www.editions.flammarion.com

07 08 09 4 3 2
ISBN: 978-2-0803-0490-2
Dépot legal: 10/2005

Printed in Italy by Canale